NO EGO

Also by Cy Wakeman

Reality-Based Leadership
The Reality-Based Rules of the Workplace

NO EGO

How Leaders Can Cut the Cost of
Workplace Drama, End Entitlement,
and Drive Big Results

CY WAKEMAN

ST. MARTIN'S PRESS NEW YORK

www.stmartins.com

Designed by Mary Wirth

The Library of Congress Cataloging-in-Publication Data
is available upon request.

ISBN 978-1-250-14406-5
ISBN 978-1-250-17148-1 (international, sold outside the U.S.,
subject to rights availability)
ISBN 978-1-250-14973-2 (ebook)

Our books may be purchased in bulk for promotional, educational, or business use. Please contact your local bookseller or the Macmillan Corporate and Premium Sales Department at 1-800-221-7945, extension 5442, or by email at MacmillanSpecialMarkets@macmillan.com.

First U.S. Edition: September 2017
First International Edition: September 2017

10 9 8 7 6 5 4 3 2

For sale in the Indian subcontinent only

I dedicate this book to all those who have shared
the field beyond Ego with me.

Richard, your unconditional love has shown me what
life beyond Ego holds, and it is stunningly beautiful.

Cathy, my soul sister, who has traveled the journey back to
"No Ego" with me many times, resulting in incredible joy.

The Reality-Based Dream Team—Ana, Alex, Sara, Ellie, and Kelli.
You are daily proof that a "No Ego" workplace is not only
possible, but truly the path by which we really can
have it all at work—happiness AND success.
By practicing what we preach on the daily,
you have delivered results beyond
even my wildest dreams!

Out beyond ideas of wrongdoing and rightdoing,
there is a field. I'll meet you there.

When the soul lies down in that grass,
the world is too full to talk about.
Ideas, language, even the phrase "each other"
    doesn't make any sense.

—MEVLANA JALALUDDIN RUMI, 13TH CENTURY

Contents

NO EGO

SHUT THE

CONVENTIONAL DOOR

My entry into Reality-Based Leadership started with the Open-Door Policy.

After several years as a family therapist, I got a promotion in my organization. For the first time, I would be leading a team, which got me a free ticket to the Human Resources boot camp for managers. Designed to prepare me for my new organizational role, it was a crash course in the current conventional wisdom around leadership.

One particularly juicy leadership gem, delivered to me by trainers with all the confidence in the world, was that a great leader always has an open door.

An open door? That was easy. Not only was I going to have an Open-Door Policy, I was going to ace it! I hustled down to the gift shop at the health center where I worked and bought a doorstop to make a visible and decorative point: I'd have the most outstanding open door in the organization.

The Open-Door Policy did exactly what it was supposed to

do. Soon team members began popping their heads into my open door.

"Do you have a minute?" they asked.

"Sure, I have two!" I'd reply. "Come on in."

It didn't take long to realize that these people were liars. They'd ask for a minute or two, but they stayed planted in my office for an average of 45 minutes.

Now, if they had really needed me—to talk through a critical decision for serving the business or to help them develop or hone skills—the time investment would have had a satisfying payoff. But people weren't coming to me for that.

People came in to tattle on others. They wanted to tell me stories about things that had happened only in their heads. Or they'd vent about circumstances that couldn't be changed (what I call reality). They'd use our time to spin fantasies about a dismal or doomed future. Frequently, it was a combination of these things. I spent the majority of these impromptu "Got a minute?" meetings listening to elaborate narratives that had almost no basis in reality.

The kicker? At the end of the meeting, they would say to me, with a straight face: "Please don't do anything about this. I just wanted you to be aware."

As I witnessed the economic effect of this Open-Door Policy in action, it made no sense to me. Where was the return on the investment I had made in that doorstop? Can you imagine what would happen if I went to the CEO and said, "I plan to spend 10 hours a day in a series of 45-minute one-on-one meetings talking about stuff that doesn't add one whit of value to the company. And I'm going to expense the doorstop"? I'd soon be opening the door to the unemployment office.

The HR wisdom that had been drilled into me said having an open door was the right thing to do. It was touted as a best practice that would lead to happy, engaged employees. We had been instructed that we should allow employees to vent, because venting is "healthy."

During my time as an Open-Door Policy devotee, I don't recall team members ever tattling on themselves. They weren't coming to me and saying "You know, I am really having trouble aligning my actions and decision making with the strategy of this business. I'd like to become more effective at serving our customers. Can you help me develop my skills and work processes so I can meet company goals, add value to the team, and better contribute to return on investment?"

No one came through my open door to directly ask for coaching on handling sticky issues in a more effective, productive, and efficient way. In fact, they drove their BMWS (bitching, moaning, and whining) through the open door and parked with their engines idling, wasting fuel and polluting the atmosphere. Then they demanded that I withhold the kind of direction and assistance that would help them get where we needed to go.

I realized pretty quickly that the open door was a portal for drama. It catered to ego, fueled feelings of victimhood, and contributed to low morale. Worse, it cost the company a lot of money. We had been hired for the value we could contribute to the important work we did, not for the ego-based, drama-filled stories we could concoct. I knew my time would be better invested in helping people reflect, increase their self-awareness, and look at situations from a higher level of consciousness.

After this proverbial "aha!" moment, I abandoned the Open-Door Policy. It was one of my first acts of Reality-Based Leadership. I didn't shut the door on my team members, exactly, but I began changing the conversation when they asked for a minute. Instead of passively listening or directing, I began asking questions:

"What do you know for sure?"

"What is your part in this?"

"What are your ideas for resolving this issue?"

"What are you doing to help?"

When they came to me with narratives about the problems they encountered, I gave them a mental process that forced them to deconstruct their "stories" and move into action. The process shifted their thinking to a focus on the facts. And it asked them to outline proposed solutions or helpful actions that would positively affect the situation.

A core philosophy of Reality-Based Leadership is Stop Judging, Start Helping. My employees always had one question on the back of their badges: "How can I help?" Whenever they came to me to tattle, I encouraged them to go directly to the person they were judging and ask "How can I help?" instead. Asking this simple, sincere question would lead to instant teamwork.

Conventional Wisdom Fail

The Open-Door Policy failure got me thinking more about the conventional wisdom that had been dispensed in my leadership training. What if what we had been taught in HR's leadership boot camps was all wrong? Based on the results we were getting, the traditional leadership methods certainly didn't seem to be working.

I could see the damage being done when employees were what I came to label "emotionally expensive." These were the folks who spent their time arguing with reality instead of confronting it directly. They contributed opinions instead of taking action. They judged others instead of offering help. They saw themselves as victims of cruel circumstances instead of recognizing that circumstances are the reality within which they must succeed.

One of the first mental processes I taught employees, adapted from my cognitive therapy background, was to edit stories and eliminate the emotional churn that muddied the waters and obscured reality. People began to learn productive ways to resolve their own issues. They began to figure out what the real business issues were and come up with productive options for tackling them. They stopped the BMW driving. It wasn't long before our team began operating in a completely different way. Although leaders in other departments were getting bogged down in constant firefighting, the teams I worked with were becoming independent, efficient, and highly engaged.

That recognition sparked in me even more introspection about the role of a leader. I began to wonder: What if a leader's role isn't to improve morale or motivate employees? What if a leader's role isn't to keep employees engaged and happy? In fact, that expectation sets up leaders for failure. They can't motivate others—people make their own choices about motivation, accountability, commitment, and happiness.

A leader would better serve the organization by refusing to foster the daily theatrics at work and by coaching employees in ways that are grounded in reality. After all, not a single budget I have ever seen or managed has a line item for Ego Management. But even my short experience with the Open-Door Policy had shown me drama and emotional waste were costing the company big time.

Costly Leakages

After more than 20 years of working with the Reality-Based philosophy and honing Reality-Based tools in hundreds of organizations, I'm excited to be writing this book because I now have research data that quantify the cost of ego-driven emotional waste. Organizations are losing billions of dollars annually.

They lose money in two ways. First, they're investing money and organizational energy in employee engagement surveys, HR initiatives, and learning-and-development programs that actually exacerbate the problems they're trying to solve. Second, organizations aren't developing leaders who have the mind-sets, methods, and tools they need to help them bypass ego and eliminate costly emotional waste.

Although I have more than 20 years of qualitative experience from consulting in hundreds of organizations, I wanted to quantify the amount of emotional waste found in typical organizations to help leaders calculate the costs of workplace drama. My company, Reality-Based Leadership, recently partnered with The Futures Company to capture data around the phenomenon that the Open-Door Policy brought to my attention.

Our research found that the average employee spends 2 hours and 26 minutes per day in drama and emotional waste.

Wages and salaries vary greatly from organization to organization, of course, but let's use a hypothetical company with 100 employees, each earning $30 an hour and working 40 hours a week. Annually, wages paid would equal $6,240,000. Based on our research on the cost of emotional waste, well over $1,794,000 would have to be written off as a loss.

Now imagine that hypothetical organization has 10 senior leaders, and each spends a minimum of 5 hours a week dealing with the drama that creates emotional waste. (And that's a conservative estimate, based on our research.) Let's give these leaders salaries that average $60 an hour. That's another $156,000 of money spent on something that has no return on investment.

Would you continue pouring money into a stock that consistently lost that kind of money? You'd be crazy to do that, but at least you're able to see when a stock is losing money. In organizations, emotional waste has been an invisible leakage, much like the slow leak in the upstairs shower that goes unnoticed until the ceiling and walls collapse and cause untold damage.

Recapturing Resources

Imagine the dramatic impact on profitability that would be seen if you could recapture the two-plus hours per employee per day expended on emotional waste. That is what the Reality-Based philosophy is all about.

Not only have organizations that we've worked with seen profound cost savings through the increase in productivity and improved results, they have seen measurable improvements in engagement, collaboration, and cross-departmental teamwork. They have been better able to retain the employees who are highly accountable, do more work with less staff, and increase innovation. They have experienced measurable improvements in organizational metrics, such as work efficiency, quality control, safety scores, and customer satisfaction.

In this book, I'll show you what is possible by sharing stories collected in my decades of work using the Reality-Based philosophy to dramatically increase employee accountability, which leads to increased engagement and improved results. Most important, this book provides easy-to-use tools and methods, which can be implemented immediately, to help you recapture the hours wasted on processing drama. It builds on the concepts in my previous books, *Reality-Based Leadership* and *Reality-Based Rules of the Workplace*. You will learn to see the science of employee engagement in a new way and understand why the ways organizations have historically measured employee engagement are fundamentally flawed. You will come to understand that the means by which most leaders seek to manage change actually fuels drama and stunts employee development.

In fact, let me tell you a story right now. It happened at a major Midwestern medical center I worked with. In a potentially disastrous situation, a leader who had Reality-Based training asked one key question that led to fast, profound change for her, the employee she was coaching, and the experience of a patient.

A nurse who had just begun her shift entered a patient's room. Her mission was to explain the surgical procedure for which the patient had been scheduled and outline the preparations that she, as the assigned nurse, would be doing. The details were contained in the electronic medical records.

Unfortunately, the nurse was explaining a procedure that the patient wasn't scheduled to have. The information on the record was incorrect, and the wrong procedure was listed.

You can imagine the drama that ensued. The patient, already fearful and anxious about having surgery, became borderline hysterical. She questioned the competency of the nurse and the hospital, as well as her decision to have the procedure in the first place. She demanded to leave.

The nurse was equally furious about being put in the position of giving bad information to a patient. Instead of trying to calm the patient down or reassure her that she would get to the bottom of it, she told the patient abruptly, "This is not acceptable! Excuse me. I'll be back." And she left the room to find her supervisor.

In an unmitigated state of fury, the nurse catapulted herself into a BMW and drove it to her supervisor's office. Loudly and angrily, she began to vent. How could admissions be so incompetent? What the [expletive] was she supposed to say to this patient? Errors like these cause patients serious harm, injury, or even death! Someone should be fired! If she, the nurse, had done her job in such a sloppy way, she surely would be. And why should she have to be the one to clean up this mess with the patient?

The leader knew the distraught patient was waiting, and there was no time for extensive coaching or problem-solving. She asked the nurse to take a deep breath or two in order to calm down a bit. She acknowledged the difficult situation. And then she asked the question: "Tell me, what would great look like right now?"

The nurse was taken aback. But to her credit, she took the question seriously.

Well, she said, "great" would be acknowledging to the patient that an error had been made and then doing her best to calm and comfort a fearful, angry person who was asking to be discharged immediately. "Great" would mean tracking down the orders for the procedure the patient was scheduled to have, with the signatures of the patient's doctors. Another way to be great would be to reassure the patient that the situation was not indicative of the quality of care she could expect from this hospital. It would mean finding the patient's doctors so they could visit the patient before the procedure and provide additional reassurance. "Great" would be doing everything in her power to serve the patient, doing her utmost to ensure the best possible outcome. And "great" would mean being helpful to other members of the healthcare team instead of criticizing and demanding someone lose his or her job.

"Good," the supervisor replied. "Then go be great."

NO EGO CORE BELIEF
Professionals give others the benefit of the
doubt—they assume noble intent.

That's what the nurse did. "Once I went back in there and responded in a way that greatness demanded, the way I think I should have in the first place, it was fine," she told her supervisor later. "I told the patient that I was happy this mix-up had been caught and I was going to take care of her and make sure she got the procedure for which she was scheduled and the best possible care. I emphasized that everyone at the medical center was committed to her care."

The patient had been grateful and reassured, and the nurse felt great about helping her get there. Everything turned out the way it should. The nurse acknowledged to the supervisor that after she had calmed down and thought about it, she realized admissions typically did a superlative job. Human errors happen, and the admissions process had been designed with a backstop in mind—it required a second check by the nurse to ensure accuracy of the records.

The nurse would benefit from a similar process backstop, as someone else would be required to check on her work to make sure the patient was safe and treated well and had a great outcome. Even so, the nurse offered to help go over the breakdown with the admissions team in an effort to prevent future errors.

The simple question "What would great look like right now?" is completely disarming. It demands that people reflect on their *own* contribution to great results. It stops emotional waste in its tracks. It relies on a positive belief that everyone is capable and smart and knows what great looks like. People often just need coaching and encouragement, in the moment, to recognize reality, move beyond their egos, and make the choices that will lead to greatness.

In our work, we tell leaders one of their principal roles is to issue "the call to greatness" and help others be great. That's the definition of leadership. Keep reading, and we'll show you how to do it.

1

DRAMA AND THE DATA

As a committed lover of reality and a student of the facts, my career has been built on deconstructing conventional wisdom and helping people stop counterproductive practices. One of the ways I do this is with scientific studies. As I do research, counterintuitive truths often emerge. When I find something to be the opposite of what I had thought was true, I get super jazzed because of the opportunities that presents.

When I was confronted with a leadership dilemma in the early 1990s, a research project (chronicled in my first book, *Reality-Based Leadership*) and an accidental discovery led me to become what I consider myself today, a drama researcher.

I was working as a clinical coordinator of several small clinics associated with a large medical center. At that time, cutting-edge technology had me excited about rocking the physicians' worlds with an electronic medical record that would make cumbersome paper charts obsolete. Physicians and staff would be able to enter their notes into a computer in real time. Genius! This technology would make doctors more efficient and give them more time to focus on patients. No longer would they have to dictate comments and wait to review transcriptions of patient notes. Patient records would be centralized and accessible to providers no matter where patients entered the medical system—via the Emergency Care department, the clinic, or hospital admissions. The technology would lead to patients getting higher-quality care with more consistency. We were making a rational move based on a well-developed business plan. Slam dunk, I thought.

Except the physicians weren't ready to have their world rocked. They were openly opposed to using the technology and skeptical about the purported time savings. This small ripple of skepticism led to waves of resistance that churned the entire system. Physicians were convinced this new tool would slow them down, so I fell back on what I knew. My team and I would gather data and see what reality said.

We created a time-study research project. I was excited about flexing my research muscles but wanted to keep the project simple. Observers were assigned to watch physicians as they worked in the exam rooms and to record time increments in one of two columns. The first column tracked the time physicians spent working directly with patients. The second documented time they spent typing notes into the computer. The data collected would allow us to compare the findings with existing data on time spent documenting patient records.

It wasn't long before the observers called to tell me they needed a third column. They insisted something was showing up that we hadn't factored in. Initially I resisted adding a third bucket of data collection because I didn't want the complication. But the third column turned out to provide the most startling revelation in the study.

The Genesis of Emotional Waste

The third column revealed that physicians spent about two hours a day kvetching about the new technology or about the patients. Many doctors even crossed the line of professionalism by complaining about their new work reality to the patients. You don't have to be an expert in research to see the problem with that.

Two hours? Physicians could have invested that time in developing their technology skills, strengthening their patient relationships, and adding value to the enterprise they had committed to serve. Physicians could have used those two hours to get ready for what was next.

In that first study, we hadn't "seen" the need to include a third column because it didn't occur to us that drama-engendered resistance to a new technology would create a major leakage in the productivity pipeline. The technology worked just fine. The resistance to the change, however, eroded the potential efficiency it was designed to create. The study made that visible.

Over the years, it has become clear to me that this study was no outlier. I have observed the same phenomenon with team after team, with department after department, and in organization after organization. Drama generates emotional waste, draining the organization's time and energy. It contributes to destroying the most considered and strategic business decisions. This is why I call myself a drama researcher, and such research has been at the heart of my work for decades.

Taking a Fresh Look

After several years of working in organizations, my team and I decided to revisit, expand, and validate that original research project. We wanted to see how things might have changed since the early 1990s and to expand our knowledge about how leaders deal with emotional waste. We partnered with The Futures Company, a company that specializes in understanding and anticipating change and identifying trends.

We surveyed 800 leaders from more than 100 companies that represent medical, technology, manufacturing, and financial organizations. For purposes of the survey, we defined "emotional waste" as "mentally wasteful thought processes or unproductive behavior that keeps leaders or their teams from delivering the highest level of results." We created questions to calculate the time leaders spend dealing with the workplace drama that generates emotional waste, behaviors such as:

1. Lack of ownership, accountability, commitment
2. Blaming circumstances or other people for lack of results
3. Arguing with circumstances that were nonnegotiable
4. Resistance to change
5. Lack of buy-in to organizational strategies
6. Spreading gossip
7. Projecting (and believing) made-up stories instead of focusing on facts

8. Defensiveness to feedback
9. Dealing with hurt feelings

The survey also sought to know whether leaders believed that dealing with those behaviors was a good use of their time. It asked whether leaders had training programs to deal with such issues and whether their efforts to stop emotional waste worked.

Organizations invest heavily in HR-sponsored initiatives such as employee engagement programs, leadership training, and other ways to increase productivity, so we also surveyed Human Resources leaders. We wanted to discover how much time HR leaders saw disappearing due to emotional waste and the kinds of drama they saw fueling it. Did they see defusing drama as a productive use of their time? Of leaders' time?

Finally, we wanted to get a vivid picture of how drama shows up. Our analysis could illuminate how much emotional waste is costing the bottom line and give us a feel for the cultural collateral damage (i.e., lowered motivation and morale) it causes.

The Headline: Emotional Waste Is Increasing

The biggest surprise that emerged from the study was that, since the 1990s, time lost in drama at work had increased. The data showed leaders were spending almost 2.5 hours a day in drama that creates emotional waste at work.

Sit with that number for a moment. Roll it around in your head.

Nearly 2.5 hours a day, more than 17 hours a week, 68 hours a month, 816 hours a year, multiplied by the number of people in your organization, is leaking out of the business. These numbers likely reveal what you already have felt at work: the wasted time, the energy drain, and the difficulty accomplishing things that shouldn't be that hard.

In the survey, leaders were asked to identify the major sources of drama that they experienced ("drama" was defined as "mentally wasteful thought processes or unproductive behaviors"). There was high agreement between the leaders' group and the HR leaders' group on major sources of drama. Based on the highest-ranked sources of drama on which they spent the most time, the responses boiled down to five major categories (a scattering of one-off listings were outliers and accounted for 10 percent of the responses, of which the highest was 3 percent and the rest were minimal):

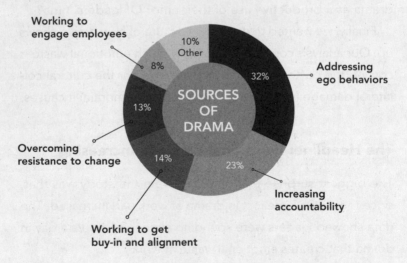

Working to engage employees — 8%

10% Other

Addressing ego behaviors — 32%

SOURCES OF DRAMA

13%

Overcoming resistance to change

14%

23%

Increasing accountability

Working to get buy-in and alignment

These are the five categories traditional leadership philosophy has concentrated on for more than 30 years. And the focus of our work at Reality-Based Leadership is to move beyond these worn-out leadership philosophies and strategies and to call for very different approaches to these sources of drama.

To reduce the amount of emotional waste in the workplace, leaders need to challenge current thinking about these five categories. The role of leadership must change so it can more effectively address the waste and drama created by these behaviors and mental processes. In addition, leaders need to be better equipped to defuse the drama driven by these main sources of emotional waste.

Leaders who become fluent in bypassing the ego will address more than 30 percent of the issues and have the biggest opportunity to eliminate waste in the workplace by facilitating No Ego Moments with their teams. The remainder of the sources of waste can be addressed by evolving the current thinking in HR and leadership development by questioning long-held beliefs and assumptions about change management, engagement, accountability, and buy-in.

Almost half of the leaders surveyed recognized that dealing with drama behaviors was not a productive use of their time. And 62 percent said they had learning and development tools and programs to deal with the issue. But in spite of such resources, *2.5 hours a day* continued to leak out of the productivity pipeline due to emotional waste.

The average worker spends 2.5 hours per day in drama.

Why is this happening? Why aren't those tools, techniques, and training working? What is preventing leaders from plugging up the leaks emotional waste generates?

Traditional tools and programs being taught and used over the last few decades simply don't work for six reasons:

1. They feed the ego.
2. They tolerate dissent to nonnegotiable strategic decisions.
3. They focus on fostering engagement but without accountability, which leads to entitlement.
4. They coddle people's preferences rather than helping them grow their business readiness.
5. They don't help employees develop better mental processes through reflection and heightened self-awareness.
6. They actually generate, rather than eliminate, emotional waste.

This list reflects the flawed logic that Human Resource philosophies and programs have been delivering to leaders for years, with serious, damaging results. Employee engagement and change management programs employed over the last three decades are broken and have proven to be counterproductive. The result has been that organizations are inadvertently creating coddled workforces that demand leaders motivate them, boost morale, and make them happy. How is that even possible?

Today's work experience is so full of emotional waste that for many people, it's seen as normal. It's considered a cost of doing business, an inevitable surtax you pay for working with complex human beings. But once our research had identified, named, and helped us understand emotional waste, it was clear that the financial impact was real. Since that time, I have devoted my career to helping people recapture the time spent on fruitless drama and redirect it to add value and great results.

Hello, My Name Is Reality. Have We Met?

We all have mental filters that distort or obscure reality and transform it into a self-serving, ego-approved story. Our stories are invented to make us look good or excuse our lack of action. They support our viewpoints so that we can get what we want. These stories make us feel safe, let us off the hook, and give us someone to blame when we don't get what we want. The mental filters are the opposite of prescription eyeglasses, which are designed to help us see more clearly.

As a therapist, I saw great benefit in helping my clients bypass ego and get acquainted with reality. We worked together to deconstruct ego-infused stories to reveal the circumstances as they truly existed.

One of my strategies was to help people find the facts rendered invisible by the mental filters they used to interpret circumstances. Their perceived unhappiness, lack of success, or reluctance to be fully engaged at work had to do with deep-seated, often subconscious desires to bend reality. For example, a frustrated client might tell me she was passed over for a deserved promotion.

I would ask, "Why do you think you didn't get the promotion?"

Well, the system is rigged.

"How is it rigged?"

Well, for one thing, my micromanager boss makes it impossible for me to be successful. He is always checking up on my work.

"What happens when he checks up?"

Well, a lot of times I am behind on my work or about to miss a deadline. But it isn't always my fault.

"What did you see the other person doing to get a promotion?"

Well, she sucked up. She stayed late and worked with other people to make sure she got her assignments done on time. In fact, she did whatever the boss asked her to do. She was always in the boss's office filling him in about her work. Oh, and she got a master's degree.

My client unwittingly listed a lot of great ways to show the boss you're ready for a promotion.

"Have you talked to the boss about what you might do to be in a better position to be promoted?"

Well . . . no, I haven't. I've been too mad.

"Maybe if you want the promotion she got, you could willingly do what she did."

What is the reality behind the lack of promotion? Was the system really rigged, or was my client's thinking stuck in ego? What might the story have been if she did her work on time, kept the boss informed on projects, and continued her education?

In organizations, HR and leadership philosophies about change management and employee engagement have been based on similar, counterproductive assumptions that allow and even encourage people to argue with reality. The thinking is that if leaders can soften the blows of change and focus on people's comfort and happiness, employees will be committed and produce better results. Many leaders and HR professionals believe that asking people what will make them feel engaged, and then meeting those demands, leads to happy, successful employees. That's another form of telling employees that great results come from changing reality. But it doesn't work. Reality can't be changed.

NO EGO CORE BELIEF
Suffering is optional and usually self-imposed.

The Leadership Buffet

Modern organizations approach leadership strategies like a buffet. Each leader often chooses his or her own HR-blessed approaches and solutions—whether evidence shows the approach to be effective or not. This approach inserts massive variance into organizations that demand tight processes based on solid evidence. It is a departure from how most companies typically manage productivity, which is to maximize resources by standardizing best practices based on data and business insights.

Human Resources has come under a lot of scrutiny and criticism in the last several years. In 2015, the *Harvard Business Review* even called for HR to be blown up. In that issue, Wharton business school professor Peter Cappelli says that HR needs to be a strong advocate for excellence. But too often, HR has been the dispenser of conventional wisdom that has only transactional or incremental impact. Our study shows that leaders don't view dealing with drama as a good use of their time or capabilities. In fact, the survey makes clear that HR resources, training, and development aren't actually solving the emotional waste problem, and most people don't realize the philosophy and tools are actually contributing to drama.

The question becomes: If companies blow up HR, what's to be done with the rubble? The *HBR* article advocated an HR "long view" that is directly connected to the pressures businesses are encountering. Reality-Based Leadership is about that: a simple approach, backed by science, using intentional mental processes and higher consciousness to reduce drama and eliminate emotional waste. That's what this book is about. Ultimately, leadership is about manifestation of the truth by directly confronting reality.

Reality-Based Leadership processes and techniques interrupt nonproductive thinking. They show people how to bypass the ego to create self-awareness, reveal new truths, and settle the mind. The easy-to-implement approaches drive big results. We show leaders how to call people to greatness, over and over again in daily conversations, to bring out something that already exists within each willing employee. As employees internalize these mental processes of RBL, they begin to self-manage, become more productive, and, as a result, understand the connection between their choices and their states of mind and the results they deliver. Anyone can achieve this, but it starts with leaders.

In the Reality-Based Leadership/Futures survey, leaders reported that 32 percent of the time they spend dealing with drama in the workplace is spent addressing what I call "ego behaviors." These include:

- Dealing with hurt feelings, misinterpretation, or speculation
- Dealing with employee hearsay or gossip
- Handling defensiveness and/or resistance to feedback
- Dealing with employees who vent or complain
- Managing workplace gossip
- Addressing employees who tattle on or judge others
- Addressing employees who compare their situations with others

These behaviors are common symptoms of the ego being engaged, bruised, chafed, or battered.

The cost of emotional waste is staggering. Ego-based resistance to change, employee disengagement, lack of alignment to strategic initiatives, and the lack of buy-in is costing companies millions of dollars per year. And while there is no lack of training, tools, and techniques available, the root causes of emotional waste haven't been dealt with.

You have the opportunity to start addressing those causes and to do so immediately.

2

EGO VERSUS REALITY

The ego is not your amigo.

The thing is, we all have one. The ego is the part of our psyche that mediates self-identity and experience, and ego is instrumental in governing how we adapt to reality. Having an ego is nothing to feel bad about. Yet it is also important to recognize that one of the ego's main functions is to generate emotional waste. It is an unreliable narrator of experience because its judging nature separates us from others. It delights in the drama it can create. The Buddha called the ego the source of all suffering.

Reality, in contrast, is your friend. It's the pal who will give it to you straight. The highest-quality data comes from reality. If you rely on reality to guide your decisions, it won't let you down. It gives you reliable, real-time information about what works, what doesn't, and where you need to grow next.

Ego and confidence are not the same thing. To have confidence is to have faith in your own abilities and believe in yourself; the ego is something else entirely. Unlike confidence, the ego operates out of self-interest. It seeks approval, accolades, and validation at all costs in order to be seen as "right." It is resistant to feedback and assigns motive that is rarely verifiable.

In the workplace, the differences between confidence and ego can make or break your career. That's because when you allow the ego to take over, bad behavior ensues. Suddenly no one can get the job done quite like you can, and all sense of teamwork goes out the window. It's one thing to work hard out of passion and a sincere dedication to results. It's an entirely different thing to take on a self-righteous attitude and judge others along the way. Having such an egocentric outlook will close your mind to new solutions and prevent you from learning the lessons at hand. Growth will soon come to a halt, as will your contributions to the organization.

You know what works harder than anything to filter out reality's lessons? Ego.

In our study, ego was at the bull's-eye of emotional waste in the workplace. It is the enemy of workplace engagement and the foe of productivity, innovation, and happiness. Ego will coax you to be one up or persuade you to be one down. One up, and you're convinced you're right, you're better than others, and people should always listen to you. One down, and you're misunderstood, helpless, and a victim of circumstances.

Another reason the ego is not your amigo? It's the enemy of profitability.

If you want to be an effective leader, you have to understand and manage the ego—both your own and that of others. Learning ways to bypass the ego helps people raise their consciousness and respond to the call to greatness. Unfortunately, this is another instance where traditional leadership techniques and tools actually have encouraged ego-driven behavior to the detriment of great results.

We already talked about one example that feeds ego—the Open-Door Policy. It invites people to drop by and vent, to tell stories that, in most cases, aren't based in reality. Venting might feel good in the moment, but it's just a way of letting the ego take the wheel. Ego loves a good ride in the BMW (bitching, moaning, and whining.)

NO EGO CORE BELIEF
Venting is the ego's way of avoiding self-reflection.

Always on high alert, ego scans the environment for fodder to create stories of anger and outrage, assault and helplessness. It nurtures seeds of dissatisfaction until they grow into a full-on burning bush. Ego is brilliant at finding insult where none is intended. I've seen it happen thousands of times in organizations, but one story in particular stands out.

We were rolling out Reality-Based Leadership in an organization, and one employee confided to me that the work environment was toxic. I hadn't seen evidence of that, so I asked her for data. She pulled up an email.

It said: "You are invited to an ice cream social at 2 p.m."

Free ice cream! In the lobby? What was I missing? "I don't get it," I told her.

"You don't know the backstory," she replied. Managers had chosen the 2 p.m. time slot for the ice cream social because it coincided with her team's peak workload. It was a plot. Management knew there was no way she and her team could enjoy a get-together at 2 p.m.

Now, I knew these leaders pretty well. I told her that I felt certain the decision making around what time to have the ice cream social wasn't based on ways to keep her team from attending.

"But you don't know the other backstory," she insisted. "I am lactose intolerant, and they don't even provide me with any substitutions."

Conspiracy and insult. This employee's ego was working overtime to generate anger over her perceived mistreatment. That is what ego lives for. Its reality filter will mislead you every time. Ego-based stories keep the emotional waste pipeline chugging along at full speed and, unfortunately for organizations, clog the flow of productivity, creativity, and innovation.

Taming a Toddler

For most people, ego is like a two-year-old who clings to a toy. Because toddlers' brains are not fully developed, trying to get something away from two-year-olds is like trying to talk ego out of its story. If you want to get toddlers to release a toy, snatching it away is a bad strategy. You'll incite a tantrum. Reason and logic don't work either. Toddlers want what they are fixated on in the moment. It is their single-minded reality. The most effective way to bypass toddlers' current attachment is to offer them something new and desirable. Doing so creates cognitive dissonance, because toddlers can't hold two desires at one time. Typically, they will drop the old toy for the new one.

Backed up by my research, at Reality-Based Leadership we've discovered that in most people's current consciousness, the ego is like a two-year-old. Traditional leadership strategies are based on how to carefully take away the toy from the toddler without sparking a tantrum. Leaders have been trained to use logic and reason in the face of an invented story or to wheedle and bargain. Leaders can invest great energy in helping others see reality, but if someone is stuck in ego, it's probably not going to work.

NO EGO CORE BELIEF
The impact of a leader does not come from what he or she *tells* team members but from what he or she gets them thinking about.

Just as two-year-olds can't focus on two things, people can't vent and self-reflect at the same time. That's where ego bypass comes in. Leaders can learn to bypass the ego through questions and tools. Doing this not only circumvents the story, it invites people to raise their consciousness by considering a fact-based reality. This is important, because leaders have been told that it's healthy to allow employees to vent, and it's not. There are three points I want to emphasize here:

1. Most people are venting about things that never happened. Sharing a feeling takes one sentence: "I feel frustrated." Everything after that is probably invented. "I feel frustrated because Steve intentionally didn't give me the information I need. He always waits until the last minute. Clearly, he doesn't value our department, and he's doing this on purpose just to sabotage me." Everything after the word "frustrated" is a story that creates suffering. It's a way to rationalize stress or anger or lack of motivation, but it's not reality.

2. Venting doesn't resolve anything. It leads to more venting and ramps up overall negativity. When

people tell me, "Yeah, but people need to vent. It makes them feel better," I always respond, "So does crack cocaine, but that's not really a good lifestyle choice." Research backs this up. Venting leads to more negative thinking, not to problem-solving.

3. The key way people grow in accountability is through self-reflection. Venting and self-reflecting are mutually exclusive. Venting leaves people stuck in ego. It stunts growth and kills accountability. Leaders who encourage, or even allow, venting are coddling employees. Doing so gives leaders the impossible responsibility of managing how others deal with change. Allowing employees to vent is a big barrier to helping them develop the skills they need to be ready for what's next. Traditional leadership strategies invest a lot of time and energy doing things that keep people unready.

The leadership trick to bypassing ego is to defuse it by engaging the part of the brain that is capable of self-reflection, cognitive analysis, and decision making based on good data. That's a big part of what we offer with Reality-Based Leadership.

It's not hard. We can teach it in one day. It can be done in the hallway, an office, the cafeteria, or at the water cooler. It doesn't involve hours and hours of one-on-one sessions or written development plans. The main thing leaders need to do to defuse ego is to start asking good questions.

Effective leaders ask questions rather than providing answers. The questions are key. Great leaders don't tell people, they don't direct people, and they don't order people around. They facilitate great thinking through self-reflection. We talked about one ego-bypass question in an earlier chapter: "What would 'great' look like?" Here are a few other ego-bypass questions:

What do you know for sure?
What would be most helpful in this situation?
What could you do next that would add value?
What could you do right now to help?
Would you rather be right or happy?
What is helpful in this situation—your expertise or
   your opinion?
How could we make this work?

A Different Approach

Questions like these can help people see more clearly and can transform the negative energy into self-reflection. Good questions can lead to greater self-awareness and positive change. They help people get working on the right things.

I used this technique with a member of my team who was stymied by a vendor group one of our clients used. What could have been a major setback for the client, and possibly our company, eventually resolved to a happy ending after one 15-minute conversation.

We were due to roll out a major training program in November. The employee who was directing the project called me in September with an update. He'd talked to the vendor's technical folks, who told him it would take at least 10 weeks to get the training program up and running. That would take the rollout to mid-December.

With its holidays and year-end distractions, December is the worst possible time to roll out training. It is such a bad time that, realistically, I knew it would push the rollout into January. The client's senior leadership team had already seen big improvements around the Reality-Based Leadership work we'd done that fall. They were eager for the entire organization to be exposed to this way of working. They knew the more quickly they could eliminate emotional waste, the more quickly they could improve business outcomes. A delay just wasn't acceptable for the business.

I told my project manager that we needed to make November work. His response was to list the reasons it couldn't. We needed the technical expertise of the client's vendor; therefore, it was a client issue and out of our control. He was enmeshed in the vendor's stories about "why we can't."

As his boss, I could have just said, "Well, figure it out. Just make it work." But that kind of abrupt, aggressive directive hooks the ego and leaves people feeling frustrated and disempowered. I wanted him to step up and develop better mental processes. In a short coaching session with real-time feedback, I asked him what he knew for sure. What could he do next that might add value? What questions could he ask the vendor's technical team that might change the energy?

He called back a couple of hours later to report. At a meeting with the vendor's technical folks, he'd suggested they stop talking about obstacles and consider "how we can." He asked: "How do you think we could make this happen on the date we promised to the senior team?" He emphasized that his question was rooted in what would be best for the client organization.

The team still complained, but one member finally said, "To make it happen, we'd have to get a special sign-off from our boss, which would take a formal request from your client."

My employee said, "Let me give them a call, and let's get a formal request going."

One phone call later, the deal was done. One question shifted the negativity of "why we can't" to "how we can." A major training program for 8,000 employees was back on schedule. Most important, the client organization wouldn't have to wait an extra two or three months to redirect emotional waste and channel that energy into getting great results.

NO EGO CORE BELIEF
Accountability is death to the ego.

Get to Know Your Ego

Ego is designed to talk you out of things, especially if you're in a discomfort zone. It doubts, suspects, rages against, and gossips about. It leads the charge on arguing with reality. It compares and keeps score: "My suffering is legitimate, but yours is not. My suffering is worse than your suffering." It overrides compassion.

Ego creates chaos because it doesn't want you to get still enough to see what is real. Reality, self-reflection, and accountability make the ego very nervous. It doesn't want to venture outside its comfort zone, so it will cling to the old and look for every possible way to torpedo change. Ego resists the things it knows will kill it. Things like:

- Mental flexibility
- Self-reflection
- Taking full accountability
- Forgiveness
- Letting go
- Moving on

Another way to avoid the ego's trap is to stop with the sympathy and use empathy instead.

Sympathy comes from a good place. We don't want to see people in pain. But sympathy exacerbates the pain rather than healing it. For instance, leaders are told to provide feedback. But typically, it is delivered in a way that engages the ego, so conflict and defensiveness result. Who likes dealing with that? In an effort to keep the peace, leaders particularly shy away from giving feedback to people with dominant egos. Instead, they offer sympathy, soothing the person's ego by agreeing and colluding with his or her self-imposed suffering.

Let me give you a typical example. Someone comes to your office after getting a memo from senior management and says, "Oh my gosh. Have you even seen this craziness? Can you believe what they're telling us to do?" It would be perfectly reasonable to say "Yes, I have. I am so glad you stopped by. Let's figure out how best to accommodate this request and minimize business disruption." Instead, you respond with sympathy.

"Oh my gosh. I know. We weren't even consulted. They are

clueless about our part of the business. They shouldn't just mandate things. This is going to really slow us down." You climb into the passenger seat of the BMW and start listing all the ways management has messed up people's lives.

SYMPATHY VERSUS EMPATHY

Too many leaders use sympathy to connect with employees. Instead, leaders should use empathy and a call to greatness. Sympathy is feeling sorry for someone, colluding with them, and agreeing with them that they are at the mercy of their circumstances. It reinforces their victim perspective. Empathy is about acknowledging their suffering and then separating out suffering from reality with a call to greatness.

Sympathy soothes the ego by agreeing with its narration and assigning blame. Empathy bypasses ego, shares an observed reality, and makes a call to greatness. Let me share a story that shows the difference.

After a long day and a late flight, I had what I jokingly call compassion fatigue. It's that exhausted state in which I don't have the energy to be nice to people. I just wanted to get off the plane, into my car, and to the hotel. Once I'd had a good night's sleep, I knew all would be good in the world again.

As I disembarked, I found myself behind a guy who soon became my archnemesis. He was trying to text on the flip phone he probably had used since high school. He would walk and stop, walk and stop, meandering left and right, foiling my attempts to pass him. My usual breathing techniques weren't keeping me calm, and it was all I could do not to push him out of the way. But just as I had that thought, he stumbled and fell off a curb at the airport. My irritation turned to concern as I rushed to help him. Fortunately, he wasn't hurt.

That incident got me reflecting about sympathy versus empathy. If I had been in sympathy mode, I might have said, "Oh, you poor thing. It's crazy that airport officials don't make it easier for us to walk and text! We should demand that curbs and other uneven surfaces be eliminated throughout the airport. How is anyone supposed to text and walk in these ridiculous conditions? Don't they want to support business travelers in Dallas?"

But an empathetic response might prompt a different insight. After I made sure my fellow passenger wasn't injured, I could have said, "Hey, so glad you're okay. Are you up for some feedback from my point of view? I was just observing that your current texting process ended up being a really painful situation. You might want to consider a phone upgrade that allows you to voice text. Not just because I think it's safer and more efficient, but if it's not easy to text here in Dallas, it's going to be impossible in a place like Mumbai. And, FYI, that is where our businesses are headed next."

Empathy acknowledges suffering, but it doesn't require collusion. It also asks people to separate what's self-inflicted from reality, which is neutral. Again, questions help create self-awareness and self-reflection: "I can see that you're struggling with reality, but I'm wondering why you're suffering because of it?"

NO EGO CORE BELIEF
Your circumstances are not the reason you can't succeed; they are the reality in which you must succeed.

I got the gift of this important lesson from a wise mentor. I was a young leader of a high-functioning team, and in one year, we were asked to move our offices several times. We muscled through the first two moves with great attitudes. Moving was inconvenient, sure, but we figured it was what the business required, and we wanted to do our share.

When we moved the third time, we all began experiencing serious headaches. After investigation, it was discovered that the new space had unacceptable lead levels. We moved a fourth time, to beautiful, but temporary, quarters while our new, permanent offices were under construction. Then came the final blow. Due to construction issues with the new building, we were asked to move again. Five times in one year. My staff was in revolt.

During a challenging meeting, my motivational speech about positive attitudes and doing our part sounded tone deaf. Team members were sick of the disruptions. They were tired of living out of boxes. They were angry at me. Why didn't I fight for them? Why didn't I point out to senior leaders that our team was full of rock stars? We shouldn't have to suffer like this.

They persuaded me to act. Full of righteousness, I marched to the CEO's office and demanded time with him—pronto. Instead, the administrative assistant called my mentor. While I waited for my meeting with the CEO, she stopped by and asked me what was going on. I told her my team was suffering and I intended to put a stop to it.

She asked: "Why is your team suffering?" I explained again: the inconvenience of the moving, the work disruptions, the unfairness of it all. And she asked again, "Yes, the reality is that you're having to move a lot. But why are your team members suffering?" Eventually the light bulb went off. We were not suffering because we were moving, we were suffering because we had refused to adapt. We hadn't grown our ability to work in different ways, to be mobile and ready for what's next.

Reality wasn't hurting us. Our unreadiness for what was next was causing our suffering. The source of our pain came from the resistance to doing what was required for the business. What would change if we developed mobility skills and the ability to quickly adapt to new working conditions?

I went back to the team and broke the news. Instead of fighting to stay stationary, we were going to get skilled at being mobile. Next time we got the call to move, we'd be willing and ready, and then it wouldn't hurt.

As long as people continue to believe that reality is hurting them, they will remain victims. If you can learn to separate suffering from reality, you can ease your own pain with readiness. Ask "Why are you suffering?" seriously. Listen closely to the answer. If suffering is based on a reality—and it usually is—acknowledge the reality and ask again: "But *why* are you suffering? It's true this project has changed significantly and requires something different of us, but what is your true source of suffering?"

Wishing that the project hadn't changed, complaining, or offering opinions about why it's a bad idea won't change the reality. Verbal suffering (venting) highlights the lack of flexibility or skills that are needed to become fluent in the now and ready to move forward. Attachment and delusion cause suffering; reality does not.

> **When asked for my absolute best advice ever, I reply, "Stop believing everything you think."**

3

A NEW ROLE FOR THE LEADER

Historically, leaders have been told their role is to inspire, to motivate, to direct, to oversee, even to micromanage. I have two things to say about that.

First, people make their own choices about motivation and inspiration, so for leaders, it's an impossible responsibility. Second, the traditional management philosophies leaders have been taught to accomplish this impossible task actually engage and enflame the ego.

The need for a leadership paradigm shift seems clear, and it makes sense for leaders to focus on eliminating emotional waste. It's just another way of doing something that is already a standard strategic business practice—improving and standardizing processes to eliminate waste. More efficient processes translate to a healthier bottom line and a more successful company. Why not apply that same business practice to eliminating the ego-driven drama that creates emotional waste? Give leaders the tools and practices they need, grounded in solid behavioral health research, to help employees develop improved mental processes.

This logical, modern approach will relieve leaders of the paternalistic burden of being all-knowing and overreaching. They can cease shouldering the responsibility of coming up with all the answers. In fostering better mental processes, leadership is no longer directive and managerial. Instead, it's centered on helping people learn to bypass their egos for the good of the organization.

This is a more effective, and respectful, way to manage others. Employees learn to see clearly that their success, or lack of it, is not up to leadership or circumstances. It is in their own hands. Leaders are relieved of the responsibility for others' choices and instead help people become experts at knowing and managing themselves. Instead of giving people answers, leaders facilitate conversations that lead people to find good answers themselves. The mark of a great leader is when employees begin using these great mental processes even when the leader is not around or no longer is in the picture. Skills, mind-sets, and competencies become portable, and employees can find success wherever they land.

The new leadership role becomes far less about managing and "making sure." It's more about energy management and facilitation. Conversations and questions are the primary tools to redirect thinking away from "perfecting circumstances" and spur thinking about how to succeed in the circumstances as they exist.

Often, for example, leaders participate in meetings as individual contributors. They offer ideas, react to others' ideas, and identify the ultimate solutions. In the paradigm I am recommending, leaders are facilitators, prompting team members to use better mental processes and collaboration to spark creativity and innovation. Discussions shift from "why we can't" to "how we can."

> **Self-reflection is the ultimate ego-bypass tool. It is also the core driver of accountability.**

Leaders can create, for themselves and for others, what I call No Ego Moments. These are opportunities to help people recognize when they're operating in ego mode. By developing an awareness of when the ego is creating its false and destructive narrative, people can be coached into settling their minds so reality can assert its power. I talked about one way of doing this in the last chapter—separating suffering from reality.

Here are other ways to disrupt ego.

> **Stop Believing Everything You Think.** Listen to your narrator. Sit quietly with your eyes closed. Do you hear that internal voice or voices? What does the conversation sound like? Do thoughts come and go without your influence? Who exactly is talking? Try jotting down what you hear in this stream

of constant thoughts. Then examine what you wrote. Ask yourself: Do I agree with what I thought? Is it true? Can I be sure?

You know ego is the narrator when you hear things like:

"I know exactly how this will play out."

"This means that . . ."

"I know it won't work because . . ."

"I was excluded . . ."

"That was unfair."

If you're embarrassed or ashamed about what you're thinking, remember you are not your thoughts. They aren't you until you give them your agreement and belief. You don't have to agree with the ego's narration. You don't even have to listen to it. You get stressed out by your thoughts only when you start believing them wholeheartedly.

———

You Go First. When you start judging others or feeling resentment about what you perceive you're not getting, turn that energy back toward your own evolution. Here's what I mean: Say you are in a discussion and are frustrated because you believe that the other person is not listening to you. As soon as you fixate on that, neither person in the conversation is listening. You have the power to fix the problem in the moment. If you think it is so easy to listen, you go first. Give to the other person what you think is missing and what you wish to receive. Break the stalemate by going first, listening intently, and being the change you wish to see in the world.

———

Open Heart, Open Mind. The heart and the mind are connected. When you open one, the other is bound to follow. When you get stuck in judgment with thoughts like *They shouldn't act that way. I would never do that. I don't act like that*, you've created an attitude of *I am right, and you are wrong. I am good, and you are bad.* Work on your mental flexibility by opening your mind. Come up with three different explanations for why someone might be behaving the way they are. What would a kinder, less suspicious, less judgmental explanation be? Then ask yourself: How am I contributing to this situation? What could I do differently to change this relationship dynamic or business outcome?

Another approach is to open your heart. For example, you can temper anger over "They lied to me" by asking "Have I ever lied to anyone?" The ability to find in ourselves what we are judging harshly in others gives us a platform for compassion and understanding. It creates a mind-set of "stop judging, start helping." This open-heart approach includes letting go of grudges. It takes a lot of energy to keep a story alive, to hold onto the past and to stay "injured." Opening up your heart is a way to release that negative energy and eliminate emotional waste.

———

Get Back on Track. When you find yourself suspicious about others' motives or behavior, it's probably a signal you should examine your own intentions and behavior. If you are confident that something dishonest or unethical is going on in your organization, by all means, report it! You *should* do something about it. Otherwise, suspicion is a good sign that you might want to be suspicious of yourself. Are you trying to control a decision? Protect your self-interest? Resist a change that would benefit you or the organization? Time spent examining your own motives often reveals that the ego is in control. If you find this to be the case, look for ways to neutralize your self-interested thoughts and actions.

Another way you can get off track is with constant thoughts or questions about quitting the job. If you're convinced the company is making you miserable and you're constantly thinking about quitting, in a way, you probably already have. At the very least, these thoughts are major distractions from the work you're being paid to do and signal your unwillingness to be fully committed. If you're telling yourself a story about why you should quit, it's a form of hiding out. You never have to be in that vulnerable position of accounting for results. If you are choosing to stay, even if it's just for today, be all in. Stay in joy. And if you really can't commit, maybe a better decision would be to go in peace.

———

Stop Guessing and Inquire. If you find yourself giving a reluctant "I guess" to these questions, why are you guessing? Get clear so you can give a full-voiced no or yes. True inquiry will lead you back to reality. The ego is suspicious of new information, even in the face of compelling evidence. Proof is the last thing the ego wants to see. The ego likes to hide out in ambiguity. Keeping things vague is a great path to a diverse bucket of arguments from which to choose. Stop guessing, do an investigation, and get clarity.

———

Take Your Own Advice. Do you have advice for others? Write down exactly what you think they should or should not be doing, and enact that advice in your own life.

———

Ego-bypass tools break projection and fuel innovation.

Tools for the New Leadership Role

If your role as leader is to facilitate the introspection and reflection that help others bypass ego in order to fertilize growth and development, how should you begin? It's not as complex or difficult as you might think. Self-reflection is a powerful way to get employees asking the true experts in their lives—themselves—for insight or advice. The expert part of oneself lies beyond the ego and can be found in quiet reflection aimed at discerning the truth. An individual who is willing to examine the truth is fostering the ability to work and succeed regardless of what the circumstances are. Discerning truth is far more effective at getting great results and helping people be ready for what's next than being directive or constantly solving people's problems for them.

> **Great leaders make reality conscious and visible so that action can be intentional, not accidental.**

A great time for giving self-reflection assignments is right after delivering feedback. Such assignments give the mind a place to start and the ego a place to rest. You can follow quick feedback by saying something like "But don't take my word for it. Check this out for yourself." This gets you, the leader, out of judgment mode and invites self-growth in the area in which the employee is feeling stressed. Stress is usually a signal for a growth opportunity.

Be sure to give the employee time to do meaningful self-inquiry, then, later, return to the conversation to see what kind of insights were gained. How did the reflection help the person account for his or her role in results? What will help the employee discover a different response in the future? What shifts in the person's thinking do you detect? The conversations will help you see where development needs and growth opportunities are. Here are a few of the questions I recommend using, followed by suggestions for more formal assignments. (See comprehensive list of questions and assignments in the appendix.)

Questions for Self-Reflection

- What are you trying to create?
- What do you want? What are you willing to do to get that?
- What do you fear that is getting in the way of action? How can you move beyond that fear or concern?
- What are some of the most challenging parts of your role? What do you wish you were more skilled or more fluent in handling?
- What part of your reality are you struggling with?
- What would happen if you just chose to agree and help?
- What would be your part in that outcome?
- What did you do that hindered? What helped?
- What do you know for sure?

- What could you do to add value?
- If you didn't have the story you're telling yourself right now, who would you be?
- What is your goal?
- How is that working for you?
- What has your current approach been? What would you like to change in that approach?
- How is the feedback I gave you true?
- If we assume the universe is kind, how might this situation be benefiting you or be for your highest good?
- What would make this successful? What will you do to ensure that?
- If there were other explanations for someone's behavior, what might they be?
- What is missing from this situation? What could you do to add it?
- What if two things are true? Where is the "and" here?

I also recommend assignments for self-reflection as a sort of crowdsourcing technique for getting more input and feedback from resources other than the leader. Such assignments are one more way of saying "Don't take my word for it." They disperse the responsibility for growth both to the employee and to those around him or her. They also give employees additional high-quality data from people with different perspectives. The assignments set the table for rich conversations and minimize the possibility of conflict. Meditation and journaling can be great supports in this area.

Here are some of the assignments we've used to great effect in Reality-Based Leadership.

Assignments for Self-Reflection

Ask or tell employees:

- Whom do you know who is generally successful under these kinds of circumstances? Connect with them, ask for their three best tips on how to be successful, and let's talk about what you learn.
- Get a clearer picture of how others experience you in meetings by using your phone or tablet to record your interactions. Watch the film and identify ways you use your body language, approach, or speech to diminish open dialogue.
- In one clear sentence, write down what you hope to accomplish or create in these circumstances. Talk to 20 people and ask them for a next step or their best tip on how to proceed. Work from that list and report back with your experience next week.
- Think about three ways this feedback could be true. Come back and share three examples of how it affected your work.
- Identify three ways that you sabotaged the work efforts. How did those behaviors or attitudes serve you?
- What are you believing? How is that influencing your choices and actions?
- Choose three people who excel in this area and interview them. Report back with what you discover.
- Write down a reality we're currently experiencing or a decision that has just been made. On a sheet of paper, write: "And this means that . . . ," then make a list of what it

means. Take a look at your list and ask, "Do you know this to be true? Can you impact this in a positive way? How might you be wrong? How does this kind of thinking keep you stuck?"

- Listen to the ego narrator in your head. Capture a day's worth of thoughts on paper. What do you notice? What themes do you see? Examine thoughts that express certainty about the future or are rooted in the past. When we reconnect, we'll talk about what sense you make of them.
- Read [a book or article] or watch [a video, TED Talk, etc.]. Identify two things that resonate with you. Afterward, let's talk about why you found those things important.

The point, and the value, in these questions and exercises is to help the employees see what kinds of choices they're making and how different choices might lead to better outcomes. The assignments are designed to help them understand that their choices won't affect reality, but their actions can certainly influence results.

The philosophy is self-study, asking yourself about yourself, getting quiet and thinking about the answers, finding clarity about what is true and where the narrator in your head is leading you astray. Insights bubble up in these conversations, and leaders are the facilitators of the self-learning. Self-reflection is a great way to grow personal accountability.

Disrupting Projection

When people feel threatened or uncomfortable, projection can be an instinctive refuge. Most people aren't even aware that it happens. Projection is a tool of the ego, used to protect itself from pain. Instead of looking inwardly for the true source of hurt and suffering, ego looks outward, eager to find someone or something else to blame. It's all too easy to mine the past for examples of wounds and injuries that trigger an emotional response in the now. Ego takes full advantage of past pain as a deflection from taking responsibility for your current suffering.

As a therapist, I frequently experienced people using projection. If a client had an emotional eruption that went way beyond the topic we were discussing, I could be confident that projection was in play, especially if the emotional charge was directed at me. Reliable signs of projection include blame, defensiveness, catastrophizing, and assigning ill will or negative motives.

Leaders need to recognize projection so they can defuse the ego and get people to clarity. Often ego confuses the person with the problem, as when someone thinks: "This leader is bringing up this issue or asking for this change, so she is to blame for me feeling at risk or uncomfortable." When the ego inspires this kind of thinking, the mind's capacity for problem-solving, innovation, creativity, engagement, and risk mitigation goes underground. When the ego is feeling threatened, it looks for something or someone to blame. And who is standing right in front of the person? You, the leader, the deliverer of news, and the instigator of change on behalf of the organization.

Projection, if it goes unaddressed, can become a default state of mind. It sparks victim thinking, low accountability, and resistance to change. People become eager to point out what's wrong and reluctant to find what they need to move forward.

Much of what happens in typical meetings is based on projection. Verbal processing is something the ego loves. If we can keep up an ongoing discussion, we can keep everything ambiguous. The ambiguity allows every ego in the room to filter the message and create a story. Yet anger, frustration, and blame need to be defused. Leaders can inspire breakthroughs by making thinking visible and concrete. Capturing the conversations in a concrete way, by using a whiteboard or flip chart, can reconnect people with reality. Alter your position from adversary to ally, change the energy by removing yourself from the discussion, and become the facilitator.

Deliver reality, then get out of the preaching and convincing mode. Stay conversational rather than confrontational. Steer employees' thinking away from the distortion of the ego's filter and into self-reflection. This is where leaders can make a big difference, by stepping up and making the call to greatness.

Creating a Conscious and Visible Reality

Teams often fall into a collective perspective of "This won't work. It's an impossible problem. I don't like this." The leader is delivering reality. The ego's arguments against reality are projected on the leader. Resistance comes in the form of doomsday predictions or sweeping generalizations. Leaders can desist with the arguing, convincing, and constant directing, which rarely works and doesn't generate commitment. In fact, it's an exercise in emotional waste.

We have created ego-bypass tools that will help you make reality, and the ways people respond to it, more conscious and visible by capturing people's thinking and verbalizing in writing.

Many of our clients have used some of these ego-bypass tools, which can be found in more detail in the appendix, to great effect.

SBAR

The SBAR tool is a useful way to help people process their stories and quickly get to the core issues. The SBAR is valuable for those Open-Door "Got a minute?" sessions. The idea is to help the employee process the story first and quickly bring you up to speed so you can provide help or approval or facilitate a decision. Leaders can more clearly see development opportunities. It's great for eliminating emotional waste and helping the employee develop great mental processes.

On a single sheet of paper, the employee should delineate the issue into four succinct points.

1. **Situation.** A concise description of the facts, minus drama. What do you know *for sure* about the current state of affairs? Leaders review, looking for accurate representation and a simple statement of the current reality.

2. **Background.** Relevant data that must be taken into account when deciding how to move forward. Leaders look for history and key information the employee is unaware of or is minimizing.

3. **Assessment.** The author analysis, which answers the question "So what?" It should highlight reasons for concern, risks, root causes, and diagnoses. In this section, leaders should look for critical thinking and

problem-solving skills and assess strengths and weaknesses. If you see development opportunities, teach by asking good questions and exploring problem-solving techniques.

4. **Recommendation.** The author's proposed action and next steps for improving or resolving the issue. The recommendation is driven by the assessment, and leaders are looking for the quality of the recommendation. Does it address the issue? Is it feasible? Is it in line with company philosophy or strategies? Leaders should work with the employee to find creative solutions and multiple options.

Negative Brainstorming

This is a great exercise for your team when it's exhibiting resistance or is in the "why we can't" mode because it will help people get unstuck. Negative brainstorming allows team members to express healthy dissent—they can get good and negative in the first part of the exercise. But eventually, the conversation is redirected in a way that asks them to step up and address the issues constructively. You'll need a whiteboard or a flip chart.

First have team members introduce their concerns, one at a time. Capture them on the whiteboard or flip chart, leaving room to write the responses of the group below each entry. Keep writing until everyone's concerns have been exhausted.

Label that chart "Risks." Point out that the team's value is its ability to mitigate risks. Ask the team to evaluate each concern or risk based on its probability—low, medium, or high. Many of the ones rated "low" are based on fear or story and can be eliminated. The heart of the exercise is to have the team create strategies to mitigate every risk labeled "medium" or "high." As team members use their knowledge and expertise to assess each concern/risk, the energy shifts to from "why we can't" to "how we can."

Thinking Inside the Box

This exercise emphasizes "and." It moves conversations to a higher consciousness level by expanding people's thinking around resources and priorities. When you hear statements about wanting to change reality, such as "We can't do this without more resources" or "We can't handle any more change," it's time to get people focused on what *is* possible within the boundaries set by circumstance. People need to understand the constraints around budget, head count, time frames, project scope, and the like. In organizations, there will always be constraints. Complaining about them or wishing them away generates emotional waste. And innovative "blue-sky thinking" where constraints aren't factored in results in wasted creativity. Suggesting a piece of equipment that provides breakthrough technology is great, but if budgets are frozen, it's not a viable way to move forward.

Another way to think inside the box is through the power of "and." Box it out and replace the "or" with "and" as you problem solve. For example, there was a conflict brewing between a group of physicians and the laboratory at the hospital. The lab wanted to process tests in batches to save time and money. The doctors wanted their results now. Waiting until the lab processed a batch was unacceptable, they said. It was an either/or stalemate. However, through the power of "and," the group came up with a solution. The doctors got a certain number of urgent requests a month and could ask for immediate results. Otherwise, they'd wait until the lab processed the tests in batches. Doctors discovered they didn't need to use their urgent requests as much as they thought, and the lab was able to operate more efficiently.

Editing Your Story

During BMW sessions, have a notepad handy so you can help people, in the moment, edit their stories. Writing down the facts as people tell their stories also can save time. If a discussion is interrupted, you can come right back to what's been created together on paper rather than trying to remember where you are after ego has had time to respin the situation back into a frenzy.

Here's an illustration of what I mean based on an interaction I had with an employee.

Lisa had asked for my advice at how to get better at training others. She was scheduled to train a group of union workers, people she wasn't accustomed to working with. I suggested that she ask them for feedback when the training was over. The day after the session, she came to me in tears, saying, "Well, I took your advice and asked for feedback." Through her tears, she related that the workers had hated the workshop. They hated the training and they shredded her abilities as a trainer. One guy had stayed for an hour afterward, writing feedback on a piece of paper.

While she spoke, I was taking notes. After she had vented and wept for about 15 minutes, I showed her what I had written:

"I asked for feedback. I received feedback. Now I am crying."

I asked her, "Are these the facts?" And she began to laugh, because they were.

Everything else was her ego-based story.

4

BROKEN ENGAGEMENT

(LET'S CALL THE WHOLE THING OFF)

In the Reality-Based Leadership/Futures Survey, leaders reported that much of their unproductive time was spent on efforts to get or keep employees "engaged."

Bad news for leaders: It's not even possible.

Engagement is a choice, not something a leader can do for others. Worse, the philosophy embedded in most engagement strategies is flawed in three dangerous ways. Typical employee engagement thinking holds these (un)truths to be self-evident:

1. Every employee opinion is equally credible.
2. Leaders must create the perfect environment for employees to give the "gift" of their work.
3. Engagement is the magic key to drive great results.

It is clear to me that we've over-rotated on engagement. To be effective, engagement has to be married to accountability. Without a strong foundation of accountability, energy spent on creating engagement will backfire and will create entitlement.

This point bears repeating: *Engagement without accountability creates entitlement.*

The philosophy of "perfecting the environment" to create employee engagement just feeds the ego and generates huge amounts of drama and emotional waste. We can't make other people happy, and this statement is backed up by plenty of scientific research. Happiness is a choice, and it's correlated to accountability. Engagement comes from the accountability individuals accept in the accumulated choices they make in the circumstances they face.

After years of using this philosophy as a therapist, I was shocked when HR told me in my first leadership position that a key part of my role was making sure my team was engaged. HR said I should give people what they needed to be happy at work. This idea was so engrained in the organization's culture that my compensation was based partly on the results of an annual employee engagement survey.

But I knew what the research around happiness said. It was super clear: Happiness is a choice. Everyone is responsible for his or her own happiness. I knew, for sure, that if "keeping people happy" meant shielding them from stress or challenging circumstances, my role as a leader would be doomed. That sounded messed up to me. In therapy, we called that "codependency."

But my reality was that I would be measured on engagement, so I would deliver. However, instead of using the conventional wisdom offered by HR, I decided to do it in ways that aligned with behavioral health research. I had three strategies:

1. Grow accountability in those people who were willing and receptive.
2. Reward and support high-accountable behavior and thinking.
3. Transition those who were consistently in a state of low accountability off my team.

I would remove the obstacles that kept highly accountable people from performing. And if an employee's love had to be purchased, that was a great opportunity for cost-cutting.

After my first year, the employee engagement survey came back with crazy results, unlike anything the HR folks had ever seen. In my department, 85 percent of the people were top-box engaged, meaning that on a scale of 1 to 5, they rated the drivers of traditional engagement a 5 in almost every category. These people were all in. They felt like I and others at work cared about them, they were satisfied with their benefits, and they were clear about the company's future direction and wanted to be part of it. They trusted leadership, and they planned to stay with the company.

The other 15 percent in my department were radically disengaged—even downright hostile. It appeared they hated me, and they hated the company. No one reported out in the middle.

Soon someone from HR was in my office: "Cy, what do you plan to do about this engagement problem you have?" Problem? We had a high-functioning team where 85 percent of the employees were excited to be working at our company. My plan was to give these employees what they needed to keep them cooking on high heat. And the other 15 percent? The way I saw it, they were working in the same exact circumstances as the 85 percent who reported being happy at work. If I couldn't fire the 15 percent who chose to be miserable, the least I could do was to make it clear what the expectations were and that they were working in the circumstances in which they had to succeed. Eighty-five percent were already doing that, and the other 15 percent could make the same choice for engagement their coworkers had. If they rejected those circumstances, I would invite them to go in peace, and then my team would be full of engaged, accountable people. They would stay accountable, and together we'd work to make the choice of engagement an easy one.

That had HR heads spinning, because their goal was low turnover. But my goal was the *right* turnover.

Breaking the Engagement

For decades, leaders have been told that they're in charge of employee engagement. They've been sold on programs and tools that will allegedly build a happy, engaged workforce. In 2015, an article on the *Harvard Business Review* blog cited a Gallup survey of 7,272 U.S. adults. Included in the results was a report that "one in two [employees] had left their job to get away from their manager." That's 50 percent. I have a hard time believing that 50 percent of employees are driven out of their jobs by leaders. In a world of no ego, employees wouldn't give leaders that kind of power.

The article said: "Given the troubling state of employee engagement in the U.S. today, it makes sense that most managers are not creating environments in which employees feel motivated or even comfortable."

To be sure, there are toxic leaders in organizations—I have worked for a couple of them—but most employees quit their jobs because they *choose* to quit their jobs. They could also make the choice to stay and learn lessons about how to work with people they find challenging. Too many people justify their decisions to quit by blaming their managers on the way out, and that is ego craziness.

This kind of engagement mind-set puts employees in passive roles. Leaders are actually encouraging employees to see themselves as victims of circumstance with the perfect excuse for not performing: "It's my boss's fault." It's like allowing students who haven't done their homework to blame the teacher for their poor grades. Leaders can't be responsible for workplace happiness. To believe they can generates a huge pipeline of emotional waste. It's time to get real about this issue.

Don't get me wrong here. Engagement, infused with accountability, is a wonderful, magical thing. Organizations need it. But the strategies leaders have been told to use to promote engagement are based on flawed logic. Based on my knowledge and work in behavioral science, I've identified three major flaws.

Flawed Logic #1: Every Person's Vote Counts the Same

This flaw becomes evident if you examine the ways organizations conduct engagement surveys. Rather than using survey techniques based on a sample size and random sampling, surveys are sent out to each employee. This sends a message that it is vital to hear from all employees and, more subtly, that every employee's opinion counts the same. Everyone's perspective is given the same value and weight. Everybody votes, and the votes are tallied and averaged to create engagement scores.

The faulty assumption here is that all employees are created equal. But they're not. If you think of how employees contribute to the organization, what value they add, you probably think of them in terms of a spectrum. The high end of the spectrum is characterized by someone like Deb the Driver, an employee who demonstrates a high degree of accountability. You communicate the expectations, set the bar, and she jumps over it every time. Not only are such employees clearing the bar, they're giving an assist to others. They offer high-value thinking and creativity, solve problems, improve processes, contribute to customer satisfaction. If leaders could, they would create a Deb the Driver clone army and sleep peacefully at night. Such employees are the 20 percent generating 80 percent of the impact in your organization.

The low end of the spectrum is characterized by someone I'll call Vickie the Victim. She wears victimhood like a beloved bathrobe and sees the world as out to get her. Complaining about coworkers and sabotaging the supervisor is one of her favorite pastimes. She doesn't like her job or the company that much, but she likes the paycheck. When she isn't meeting expectations, she makes it clear it is because someone or something prevented her from doing her work. On the rare occasion she does step up, she wants an occasion to be made of it—gold stickers and a parade. She demands at least an average rating on her personal evaluations and the raise that goes with it. Because it's easier to cave in than succumb to her drama, she gets it. Leaders let people like Vickie hang around but don't see much evidence of her work. She should have been fired long ago, but no one ever managed to get around to it. And although the Vickies probably aren't in the majority, there are probably more than anyone likes to acknowledge.

If you're going to ask for feedback on how to improve the business, whose feedback is more valuable, Deb's or Vickie's?

That's a rhetorical question. Of course, you'd be more interested in what Deb has to say. Deb sees the organization as her own. That's how she approaches her work. She's likely to have better insights on how to improve the environment for all employees.

If you solicit the same feedback from Vickie, you're likely to get a laundry list on how you could make her work life more comfortable. She's focused on her comfort zone, not on the business's needs. Why would we give Vickie's opinion as much weight as Deb's? When people tell me we shouldn't differentiate among employees in a survey process, I have to ask: "Why not?" We differentiate at work all the time. We differentiate in the hiring process. We differentiate job responsibilities, workload, salary, whom we promote, whom we fire, and whom we invest in for development. Why wouldn't we differentiate in an employee engagement survey?

This notion that all opinions have the same value is the first thing that needs to change. If we really want our engagement surveys to drive workplace results, then we need to be honest. Not all employees contribute equally, and the feedback they offer isn't equal either. Treating all feedback equally is crazy.

While doing employee engagement research in conjunction with my work on a behavioral health unit, I saw this difference in action. After we got engagement survey results back, I wanted to plan for ways that I could best support each employee and help them support each other. I asked my assistant to divide the employees on my team into two groups based on previous, unrelated research we had on employees' accountability levels. And I asked her not to tell me which group was which.

I asked the first group: "What can be done to make your workplace better? What do you want? What do you need? What do you suggest or recommend?"

Members of the first group had a list. They said their engagement would improve if I could make sure that when the pharmaceutical reps brought food in for the doctors, the company provide food for them as well. They wanted in-house daycare and flexible work hours. They recommended that the hospital pay for their scrubs and provide free parking. They had a long list of things that, quite frankly, would have made their lives a lot easier. Nothing about the list was offensive. It would have been cool to provide those things.

And then I posed the same questions to the second group. Their first response was "Oh my gosh, can you please get us a new printer on 6 Southwest?" That was a patient care floor. "The problem is, the paper keeps getting stuck in the printer, and it scrunches up in the exact place where the warnings about the blood-thinning drugs are. We're really frightened a printer malfunction could lead to a medication error and harm one of our patients. Also, we want to change visiting hours in the intensive care unit. Right now, they're based on the convenience of the nurses. But the families end up waiting 50 minutes for a 10-minute visit with their loved one, and it's exhausting for them. Plus, we know from the research that having families in the rooms can actually speed the healing process. We think the more quickly families are reunited and can be involved in the care, the better outcomes we're going to have. It would be a lot better for our patients."

I don't have to tell you which group was which, do I? It's clear which group had the low-accountable employees and which had the high-accountable ones. One group focused on how to make their own lives better; the other focused on the ways they could help their patients.

Now, don't get me wrong here. If high-accountable people say they need something to do even better work, including in-house daycare or free parking, I am willing to work with them to get that. I want to reward and retain highly accountable employees. But when you're hearing that such changes would be a down payment on their love and commitment, that's a different story. The list will never end, which creates a downward spiral. I know one company that, in response to an employee engagement survey, installed a basketball court. You know what happened after it was built? Some employees complained that the basketball hoops were painted in the colors of a professional basketball team they didn't like.

The opinions of highly accountable employees should carry more weight. It's a differentiation worth making. They're fluent in the now, and they want to be ready for what's next. Working to give them what they need is a great investment.

Flawed Logic #2: Perfecting Employee Circumstances Will Drive Engagement

Survey questions that ask about circumstances are asking employees to rate their external work environment. Questions like "Do you have all the tools you need?" or "Do you see your pay and benefits as competitive?" are invitations for people to offer up excuses for why they shouldn't choose to be committed or accountable.

Typically, survey results get compiled into a list of "action items" that equate to a long to-do list for leaders. The list catalogs ways leaders can change reality to make it as easy as possible for employees to give the "gift" of productive work. Leaders get busy trying to "fix" what employees say is broken, and the list becomes a condition of buy-in. (See more in Chapter 9, "Buy-in.")

Let me give you an example that hits close to (my) home. Let's just say I happen to know a college student who is underperforming at school, specifically in the area of writing papers and submitting them by the deadline. Or maybe they get submitted, but they're not of the quality that is going to get this student decent grades.

Using the principles of a traditional engagement survey, I would ask this student about his circumstances. What does he need in order to submit high-quality papers on time? Does he have the right tools and environment to get his work done? Does he feel loved and supported? Do his parents and professors recognize and reward him adequately? Is he clear that his parents and professors are committed to his development? Does he get along with his fellow students?

Any college student would be able to come up with a pretty good list of what he needs to succeed. (I know mine ~~did~~ would.) The list would be something like this: "Well, I could really use an upgraded laptop. And if you could up my food allowance so I can order pizza instead of having to use the cafeteria, that would save time. And could you talk to my girlfriend and tell her not to pick fights with me so I can focus on school? If you would pay for a personal tutor, I wouldn't have to schlep to the Learning Resources Center to get help. We should also invest in a better chair or a beanbag or something so I can be really comfortable when I'm writing my papers. Better lighting and good speakers to play music would really help me stay focused. And finally, my professor should send more reminders about deadlines."

This could go on and on, right? The list would get longer and longer as the student finds ways to make his life easier. And if, as a parent, I actually meet his demands, would that guarantee that he would submit high-quality papers on time and improve his grades? If you haven't lived with a teenager or college student, take it from someone who has. The answer is no. The choice to write better papers is more likely going to be aligned with natural consequences, like a failing grade or having to re-take a needed class. The student's competency in paper writing will be driven by his interactions with a reality that says his professor won't accept a late paper or that his parent won't pay for classes in which he doesn't score a C or higher.

His circumstances are not the cause of his poor grades. If his parents and professors refuse to shield him from the reality of what it takes to earn good grades, he is more likely to perform. And agreeing to the student's to-do list just creates entitlement. He'll always be able to come up with one more thing he needs in order to get a better grade.

Circumstances often are difficult. Our instinctive, very human reaction to adversity usually isn't to step up. Our first impulse is to want to quit, at least in our minds. I know I have done that 1,000 times after a really bad day or when things aren't going the way I think they should. Fantasies about finding a "perfect" new job or winning the lottery dance in my head. Mentally, we've resigned, but physically, we keep showing up at work in our BMWs.

We've set up whole departments at work to deal with the bitching, moaning, and whining that goes on, and it's called Employee Relations. This is the place where, many times, low-accountability people who have quit in their heads, yet still appear at work, go to complain about everything that's going on around them. Their ego-based complaints center on their circumstances. They bitch about their colleagues, and they whine about unfair treatment from their managers or peers, and they moan about how their circumstances thwart their ability to deliver results. And often, these complaints bring action, which trains them to believe that the job of a manager or HR professional is to keep them happy.

NO EGO CORE BELIEF
Engagement without accountability creates entitlement.

In fact, the truly valuable service that Employee Relations should (and does) provide, such as shutting down illegal, show-stopping actions like bullying, discrimination, and harassment, gets sidetracked. The job of those in Employee Relations is not to bend reality for people who are stuck in ego and don't like the circumstances—the same circumstances in which their colleagues and managers seem to be performing just fine.

Resilient, agile, and personally accountable people are better equipped to deal with the random shocks that might disrupt the system. They are the ones succeeding in the face of the circumstances they meet. And when they do complain, they should be taken more seriously because they are highly accountable.

It's past time to start thinking about things a little differently.

Flawed Logic #3: Engagement Drives Results

Most organizations have put a lot of money and time into engagement programs with the belief they will drive higher performance and better results. In the last couple of decades, I've heard people in organizations talk about their "employee engagement scores" as if they were the Holy Grail. If the scores are high, that's considered success. I see another faulty assumption there.

When I ask HR professionals and leaders across the country why they do employee engagement surveys, this simple question elicits answers like "We want our employees to be happy" or "We want to see how we're doing on employee satisfaction in the workplace" or "We want to know how our people feel." Sometimes they say good scores will help them attract the best talent or retain their best and brightest employees. But the reason engagement surveys were created and endorsed in the first place was in the hopes of driving great business results. HR, based on the answers I get, seems to have lost that point.

When traditional engagement surveys were first proposed, their advocates staked a claim that engagement was the magic key that drove results. And people have continued to believe that, but it's an assumption I question. Although there is a correlation between engagement and performance, it's not necessarily a causal relationship.

The reason we want engaged employees is to produce a better-quality outcome for the organization, to create great business results. Any other goal means we're pointed in the wrong direction. Unless engagement is sharply focused on great business results, what's the point?

One of my former clients, a director of talent for an asset recovery business with several hundred employees, was directing a "turn-around initiative." The company was struggling, and leaders knew that to survive, they'd have to make changes. They examined work processes in order to improve them. HR wanted to be part of the solution. As long as the organization was looking at processes, HR leaders recommended an employee engagement survey to get employees' views.

The company purchased a traditional engagement survey from a marketplace vendor and implemented a multiyear survey strategy. Year One would provide a baseline and benchmarks. In the first year, leaders worked with survey results, discussed action plans with their teams, and developed strategies for improvement. They worked the engagement process diligently. In Year Two, they got back good results—engagement scores were higher, company performance had increased, and everyone celebrated.

In Year Two, we began working with the company using Reality-Based Leadership philosophies, which included a hefty dose of hardwiring accountability into the workforce. It was a full-on culture shift. The same engagement survey process was used, but this time, managers combined engagement planning with an emphasis on employees' accountability to produce good results. In Year Three, engagement scores went down, a surprising and frustrating turn of events. But the shocking thing was that even though engagement scores went down, company performance improved dramatically, beyond expectations. Though people had expected that lower engagement scores would result in low performance, the exact opposite happened.

It was a head-scratcher. People were asking "What is wrong with this picture?" They had come to believe that engagement and performance were inextricably linked. My reaction? I was thrilled, because the results provided additional evidence about the flaw in the conventional wisdom I had been fighting against. The findings mirrored my experience in the organization where I had worked previously, providing more data that engagement is *not* the driver of results. As people who were disengaged—and who were being held accountable for that— left the company, performance continued to improve, and engagement scores went back up.

In the healthcare arena, I've heard people say things like "If I push my nurses too hard to meet established standards and deliver state-of-the-art care, I'll get dinged on my engagement survey." That says to me that some leaders see accountability and engagement as mutually exclusive. And that also could allow employees to use engagement scores as emotional blackmail. Even accreditation organizations look at engagement to determine the health of the organization. But they aren't asking the right question. The engagement of whom? If I'm engaging my least-skilled and least-accountable employees, does the fact they love working there contribute to the success of the company?

I'll say it again: Engaged employees are an invaluable asset. But the key question is not "Is employee engagement good?" but rather "Does employee engagement truly drive results?" It's not engagement but *accountability* that gets the credit for good results.

The example I often use to demonstrate this is something I learned in a beginning statistics class. We were taught the importance of differentiating between correlation and causation.

Did you know that the old wives' tale that storks bring babies was based on statistics? Many years ago, people in northern Europe discovered that when stork populations increased, so did the human birth rate. This finding was studied, and the correlation was strong. When the stork population increased 10 percent, so did the human birth rate. If it declined by 6 percent, so did the number of human babies. How could this be coincidence?

People began to assume that more storks meant more babies and vice versa. We can sit here today and say, "But that's ridiculous!" because we know that's not how it works. But they saw the correlation and assumed a cause.

It wasn't until years later that researchers factored in a third phenomenon, which was the quality of the food harvest. Migratory birds like storks will go where food is abundant. When northern Europe had a great harvest, the storks appeared. And it turns out that a great harvest also made human beings happy, and there would be a lot of merrymaking, including drinking alcohol and taking part in other kinds of activities that led to babies appearing nine months later. In addition, better maternal nutrition led to higher live birth rates. Turns out that the storks didn't bring the babies—the great harvest attracted storks and provided the conditions that accelerated the birth rate.

It's not engagement (storks) that is driving performance (babies)—it's the great harvest of accountability. By cultivating personal accountability, you can affect engagement, personal performance, *and* business results. In the next chapter, I'll talk about how to do it.

5

THE HAPPY MARRIAGE OF
ACCOUNTABILITY AND
ENGAGEMENT

The flawed logic and erroneous assumptions that have driven traditional engagement policies and programs have been unpacked. I've made the case for how organizations have made things worse in the ways they try to create engagement. The burning-hot question is: What do we do instead?

At the risk of being overly repetitious, I have to say it again: Engaged employees are essential to creating great results. I don't want to lose sight of that, and neither should you. But if you want to make a change, a great place to start is with employee engagement surveys themselves.

These surveys haven't been good investments or effective tools in eliminating drama and emotional waste, for all the reasons outlined in the last chapter. The good news is that you don't necessarily have to scrap your engagement survey or other efforts altogether. You just need to start looking at the data using an accountability decoder ring of sorts.

In a nutshell, organizations can use engagement surveys to raise overall accountability by attending to issues brought to light by those identified as high and medium accountables. That data can be viewed with more credibility, and those are the folks you want to satisfy. Their feedback gives you a better idea of where to invest in improvements. You can downplay things identified by low-accountability employees so as not to unfairly indict the entire organization or those who lead it. The key is knowing which responses are coming from what camps. I have found a way to get a more sophisticated and realistic analysis on the engagement data by filtering for accountability. Doing so helps you distinguish between personal accountability issues and what can be improved with changes in organizational infrastructure, resources, management, or leadership.

For example, an organization in the throes of change might have high numbers of people who aren't ready for what's next. Traditional surveys give them a tool to anonymously ding their leaders for decisions, strategy, and actions that don't fit their preferences—even if those decisions are absolutely necessary to make or keep the business competitive. Those kinds of responses show an accountability issue, not an organizational issue.

Reengineering Engagement Surveys

How do we fix engagement surveys? Let's start by looking at the ways they are used.

The first way is to measure engagement and use the feedback to guide leaders on strategies for improvement. The focus is typically on external factors (environment). The result is investment in the development or tweaking of programs, activities, tools, and the like to boost employee engagement scores. However, the variance in respondents' levels of accountability corrupts the unsophisticated way those scores are being measured.

Here's why: If people's engagement is based on external realities, behavioral science would say they have an external locus of control. That is likely to translate into low accountability and engagement that is tied to the uncontrollable variables in the environment. Indeed, dissatisfaction levels could be exaggerated by the data from employees who lack the ability or competency to respond to changing circumstances.

My research and experience in engagement has shown that addressing issues tied to external factors is a high-risk, resource-intensive strategy. Organizations end up investing a lot of effort and resources that address "feelings" rather than business reality. They are trying to treat a symptom without understanding the cause. A focus on external factors won't drive employee engagement or satisfaction in a sustainable way.

Engagement survey data also get used for organizational recognition or as part of accreditation. When engagement scores are not tied to consistently improving business results, an invisible danger lurks. If engagement scores reveal that your least-competent and least-ready employees are comfortable or highly satisfied, that's a serious business problem. If those scores are used for accreditation, especially in industries like health care or education, they don't show whether the patients or students are getting the best, most progressive care or attention. We need to factor in the great harvest of accountability so people don't get sucked into thinking that storks (engagement scores) are bringing babies (great business results).

> **NO EGO CORE BELIEF**
> **Your happiness/engagement is not correlated to your circumstances but to the amount of accountability you take for your circumstances.**

There's a lot at stake for an organization. Engagement scores often lead to big investments in the wrong things or in establishing credentials that aren't really credible. It's great to say your workforce is engaged, but is it highly accountable? Are the right people being listened to? Do the ways people engage in the organization lead to outstanding outcomes? In organizations where lots of change is happening, engagement surveys that give everyone's opinion equal weight are especially skewed. They likely will point to dissatisfaction with leadership or the organization that is based on discomfort and lack of buy-in on the individual level.

On the flip side, if you have high engagement among people who are low in accountability and who have competence deficiencies, the business will become unsustainable. Such employees might like their working conditions, but they aren't necessarily driving good results.

Over the years, I could see a critical need to develop a more sophisticated survey that filtered engagement data through the lens of accountability. With this filter, we could clean up the data and listen to the right people, work on the right things, and engage the right groups.

People often ask me, "Is it really possible to measure accountability?" It is.

Measuring Accountability

Since the 1980s, the behavioral sciences have assessed accountability with validity and reliability by using locus of control, which distinguishes between the perception of external control and internal control. That's where I started. I took questions that assessed locus of control and adapted them to the workplace as a way of measuring accountability. Doing this created a more sophisticated survey and data that were more useful. Our Reality-Based Engagement Survey has been validated using scientific methods, and we've been using it for more than six years. In dozens of companies, the results have lifted a lot of eyebrows and, more important, resulted in changes that strengthened the workforce and business results. Over time, organizations with higher levels of personal accountability scores show less variance in engagement scores, even in the face of major changes and disruption in their markets and industries.

Generally speaking, people who attribute their results to environment or circumstances are viewed as having an external locus of control. They tend to believe they have little power or influence in their successes or failures. People who view outcomes as being influenced by their own choices and action have an internal locus of control. They're more likely to take responsibility for whatever happens. And they're more likely to be resilient in the face of ongoing change.

Our Reality-Based Survey takes the traditional engagement survey questions and adds an "accountability" filter that shows how people with low, medium, and high accountability scores answer each question. The filter was built on highly validated locus-of-control research and adapted to the workplace to measure workplace accountability.

Our filter was validated with more than 200,000 people. When used with traditional engagement surveys, it turns down the volume on low-accountability feedback and tunes in to the voices of the high accountables. Our research has shown that better outcomes aren't necessarily driven by higher levels of engagement and that higher engagement is not necessarily driven by external environments. Once you can hear, loud and clear, the feedback coming from highly accountable employees, efforts to improve engagement become more robust. You can address accountability levels of the people, for instance, rather than invest in environmental changes that are susceptible to marketplace changes and might not make a difference.

Here's a story to illustrate. At one company I worked with, the results based on traditional engagement survey questions showed employees didn't trust leadership. The scores were so low that if the company had used those results to make decisions, it would have sent all the leaders to trust boot camp, maybe even fired them.

But after adding the filter, which sorts data by accountability levels, the same data said something completely different.

Among high accountables, there was high trust in the leaders, and the company's leadership was seen as a strength. Almost universally, negative trust scores were coming from low-accountable employees who saw leadership as making radical decisions and moving too fast. It was the people who weren't ready for what is next who were dissatisfied, not the ones who were eager to make progress. That's why the accountability factor is so powerful. It helps you listen to the right people.

The Magic of Visible Accountability

Our survey tool asks additional questions that help determine level of commitment, resilience, openness to learning, and amount of ownership that people are willing to take for results. Questions are validated to measure actual beliefs and mind-sets correlated with accountability. For instance, using a Likert scale from 1 to 6, with 1 representing strong disagreement and 6 signifying strong agreement, we ask people to rate them-selves on statements like these:

> The difference between success and failure is
> commitment.
> My coworkers' behavior prevents me from doing
> my best work.
> My manager should provide me all the information
> I need to do my job.
> When employees have a problem, their manager
> should try to fix it.
> An individual is responsible for learning what they
> need to be successful.

The resulting data, our clients have told us, are like "waving a magic wand" over traditional engagement feedback, revealing important information that was previously hidden. Survey results have more potential for high impact, because leaders can see where the feedback is coming from and what needs to be done to please the people who are driving success. Survey respondents are anonymous, of course, so individuals aren't labeled "low accountable" or "high accountable." (And honestly, don't you already know who most of those people are?) But the findings illuminate the accountability of teams and the organization as a whole. The results clean up the data corruption so leaders can clearly see which issues need to be addressed systemically and which need to be confronted at the individual level. Systemically, leaders might need to invest in the tools that allow high accountables to work more effectively. Individually, leaders can address accountability through better coaching, performance management, or hiring practices. That is where leaders say "Wow!" The findings eliminate drama from the equations and facilitate better diagnoses and decisions.

Instead of using survey data to jump to the conclusion that the organization isn't giving people what they need to succeed, other questions need to be asked. These include: How can we address the individual competence and lack of readiness issues in our organization? How can we address the organizational issues identified by high accountables? What action do we take that drives improved business results? Leaders also can be clear and firm about the unavailability of the third option, which is when employees refuse to be accountable while continuing to collect a paycheck. Those who aren't willing to grow and learn can be managed out, invited to go in peace rather than placated through additional investment in resources.

In the company mentioned above, we discovered that 98 percent of highly accountable employees endorsed leadership as "trustworthy." But most people in the organization fell into the low to middle range of accountability. Among low-accountable employees, 82 percent said they had extremely low trust in leadership. Developing strategies to build trust with people who didn't see themselves as accountable for business results would be foolish. The people who were driving performance already trusted the leaders. The major breakthrough for the organization was that it could stop focusing on trust earned and instead see the trust that was given.

Leaders realized their actions wouldn't please all the people all the time. The same actions and strategies won't please both the high accountables and the low accountables at the same time. Some people were going to choose to be pissed off. It only made sense to base decision making on the feedback from highly accountable people.

Can you see the difference? Without the filter, the company would invest in trying to please the wrong people, people whose egos were driving a desire for perfect circumstances. Even worse: Without factoring in accountability, the company would give complaints from low accountables the power to stop the progress needed to keep it competitive. The company's emotional waste would continue unabated.

If, however, you're hearing dissatisfaction from your highly accountable employees, you want to pay attention to that. They're doing their part and are committed to good work. They're identifying barriers or obstacles at the organizational level. Unless those problems are addressed, you could end up losing the best folks in your workforce.

From Transaction to Transformation

We worked with a new Human Resources director at a large regional credit union who had been asked to conduct a company-wide employee engagement survey. The credit union had implemented an initiative to shape the culture, with an emphasis on treating customers and each other well. An "internal service" survey, which was linked to performance reviews, was used to provide performance feedback to employees. But many employees disliked the survey and viewed the results as a kind of popularity contest. Instead of increased collaboration, it was inspiring a lot of finger-pointing. Things had degenerated to the point that the survey was filled with complaints at the personal level and judgments about coworkers, such as "So-and-so doesn't even say hello to me in the mornings."

The HR director was searching for a different approach. He had read my first book, *Reality-Based Leadership*, in which I first identified the issues with traditional engagement approaches. We came in and, with great enthusiasm, the credit union's leaders embarked on the survey process using our Reality-Based Engagement Survey. They supported the effort with a large internal PR campaign, trying to generate excitement among employees. Although not every vote would be valued equally, leaders wanted a high response rate so that they could get an accurate read on the current state of the company culture.

The response rate was great—88 percent—but leaders were disappointed in the results. Although leaders had used every conceivable communication channel—emails, meetings, town halls, corporate newsletters—to saturate the company with an "internal service" message, it clearly wasn't resonating with employees. People saw it as "flavor of the month" and figured it would eventually go away. The survey also revealed low trust in leadership and in each other and dissatisfaction with company benefits. Overwhelmingly, employees said they were upset that leadership wasn't consulting them on organizational direction, key decisions, and strategies. Scores were low in engagement *and* accountability.

Although leaders were frustrated and discouraged, they were smart enough to hear the wake-up call. Changes needed to be made, and they faced a tough choice: Did they focus on engagement or accountability? They went with accountability.

Instead of changing benefits and trying to buy people's love, they researched how competitive the credit union was in terms of benefits. After seeing data that showed the credit union offered a competitive package, leaders focused efforts on education. During mandatory meetings in the open enrollment period for benefits, employees were given detailed explanations of what their benefits were, what they truly cost the company, and why they had been chosen. Employees were shown the comparative cost in the open marketplace. Complaints about benefits subsided significantly.

Leaders also began using Reality-Based techniques, many of which are outlined in my previous two books, to address the low accountability in the organization, including among leadership ranks. They discarded the idea of a conventional HR communication campaign that said "Trust us!" Instead, leaders begin to change the conversation. For example, they made it clear that while they cared about the people who worked there, it didn't make sense to run the business in a way that required them to consult employees on every decision. Decisions couldn't, and wouldn't, be made by committee. However, they got more clear and direct in communicating what decisions were made and why. Leaders would say, "While we value you, given the direction of the market and competition, we had to make the best decision for the business and our members (customers). You can add value right now by using your expertise to shape how we successfully execute on our decisions."

Leaders began having tough, direct conversations with employees about their levels of commitment, making it clear that there were two options: Buy in or develop a plan to buy in, or decide how you're going to transition out. There was no third option. Leaders would coach people up or coach them out.

Leaders began asking questions like these: Can I count on you to be committed? Are you on board here? And if not, what's your plan to get on board? When longtime employees complained about change and threatened to leave, they were met with tough love: "We really value what you've done for the company in the past, but this is the direction we're going in now. We'd love to have you on board. What can you commit to?"

Within two years, the percentage of high-accountable employees increased 23 percent, and satisfaction among the high- and midlevel-accountable employees increased in 8 out of 10 categories. Four years later, satisfaction among high- and midlevel accountables increased in all 10 categories. From 2014 to 2016, the company saw a 50 percent reduction in disengaged employees.

The HR director told us driving engagement through accountability was hard work—work that had to be done every day: "You can't take your eye off of it. It's a daily practice. It's about hardwiring accountability into each and every climate— eventually turning the culture, not leadership heroics. When you hear a complaint that someone isn't getting the recognition they need, you ask, 'What can *you* do to get the recognition you need?' When an employee complains about a colleague, you ask, 'What is your part in this? How can you be of service? What would great look like in this situation?' "

And the business results? After focusing on accountability, the credit union exceeded its retail goals two years in a row. It exceeded its goals on performance management reviews. As low-accountability employees left, accountability scores and business metrics began to rise. The company worked with an independent consultant to measure customer impressions of the business and scored 98 percent with its customers on engagement and transparent communication.

"We stopped trying to perfect people's circumstances," the HR director said. "Our engagement improved after we used these ego-bypass techniques and started having better conversations. We increased engagement by focusing on accountability."

How to Reap the Great Harvest

I hope that, by now, it's clear that a focus on accountability is the way to move an organization forward in a sustainable way. Changing the employee engagement survey is a good place to start, but there are five things you can do right now to build accountability into your workforce and connect engagement to outstanding organizational results.

1. **Stop coddling and start listening to the right people.** Once you acknowledge that not all employees' opinions have equal value, you're on your way to engaging the right people. The numbers reflected in your engagement scores don't mean much unless you use the survey data to create high-impact organizational results. Differentiating opinions in order to understand the value of high-accountable employees and turn down the volume on low-accountable employees will help you see where your efforts need to be focused. You want to support those who are accountable and find ways to coach the others up or let them go. Efforts to engage employees who are low in accountability will create a lot of additional emotional waste. Zeroing in on accountability will help them step up or make it clear their drama won't fly in the organization.

2. **Focus on the right list.** If you aren't able to filter for accountability in your survey, do it in the postsurvey action planning. Make it clear you're not there to create perfect circumstances but to boost levels of shared accountability. Share survey results with the employees you know are driving great results, because you *know* who many of them are, even without survey data. Ask them what items on the list resonate with them. Do the problems identified by

the survey truly seem like problems to your highly accountable employees? This approach is a version of getting a second opinion and a fresh perspective, and you're getting it from a credible source. If they say some of the things on the list aren't an issue for them, take them seriously and set the issues aside. The votes of self-proclaimed victims should have far less value than the votes of highly accountable employees.

3. **Do action planning differently.** This is where you can make it clear that employees share accountability for their own experiences. Instead of asking employees "What can the organization—or I as a leader—do to help you improve your engagement?" shift the focus to ask more simply, "What would you like to be different in your workplace?" Once you have a list, take it further and ask another, more important question: "What are you willing to do to get these things?" On its own, the first question will likely generate a long list focused on requests from the organization, the manager, or teammates: "Here is the list of things I would like to see changed." The additional question puts accountability into the mix. It ups the ante, making clear that success is about shared accountability. The question helps people see they are accountable for their own optimism, energy, and enthusiasm. To what extent are they participating? In the end, a leader can't take full responsibility for an employee's engagement. If employees say they want more transparency, flex

hours, bigger offices, or free lunch every Wednesday, asking "What are you willing to do to get that?" gets at their role in making it happen. They take responsibility. Finally, find out what, as their leader, you can do to help facilitate what they are requesting and are willing to share responsibility for.

4. **Work with the willing.** Without apology, invest the bulk of your time and energy in your best and brightest and those who are willing to get there. Use the survey to look at what high accountables are saying works well and ferociously protect that. Look at where they see problems that can be fixed, and enlist their help in fixing those problems. When you up the ante for your drivers, they will reward you with an even higher level of engagement that has a true impact on organizational success. It also sends a message to the organization about who is getting the attention, and that is who *should* be getting the attention. It's not that different from what happens at home—when misbehavior gets all the parental attention, kids understand that misbehavior is the way to go. Instead, zero in on the people who are driving the business forward. Listen to them. Reward them. Doing so will either inspire others to play at a different level or make it clear they're not a good fit in your organization.

5. **Remove disengagement as an option.** Survey results are a snapshot in time. Typical engagement benchmarks suggest that 20 percent of the employee population is highly engaged, 65 percent is

disengaged, and 15 percent are highly disengaged (and still collecting a paycheck). In some organizations, leaders meet that last number with an organizational shrug, as if it were inevitable. I want to push back on that. If people aren't willing to give full engagement, why is it acceptable to demand a full paycheck and benefits? Provide managers the training, coaching, support, and permission to have tough conversations with team members. If they have clearly disengaged employees, call it out: "Hey, John, it doesn't appear like you are really engaged here. We need to talk about that." You're likely to hear excuses for why John feels disengaged, but it's essential that managers don't take on the burden of John's choice. The most effective way to get disengaged people to make a different decision is to really hold them accountable for the decision they are making. They have made a decision to disengage. That decision is renewed every day. The question you can pose to them is "What is your plan to get reengaged?" Let John tell you what his plan is. And if he can't come up with one, make sure he knows the third option—staying without being engaged—is off the table.

If you want to drive results, it doesn't make sense to support people who are open about their disdain and actively engaged in blocking progress. The actively disengaged generate the most toxic emotional waste. Work more efficiently by redirecting your engagement efforts to the people who are willing to acknowledge that accountability is their job, not the job of HR or leaders.

Stop trying to create a perfect workplace. Change, conflict, challenges, disagreements, discomfort, and frustration are all part of the price of workplace participation. And that's good news! As it turns out, humans can't be happy and engaged without struggle and strife. Without obstacles and mistakes, it would be impossible to feel a sense of accomplishment or experience professional and personal growth. Instead of removing healthy hurdles for your employees, coach them to make the leap.

In the Reality-Based Leadership/Futures Survey, 23 percent of the drama that leaders reported as creating waste in the workplace stemmed from the time they invested in dealing with issues of low accountability. Items included:

- **Dealing with employees who blame challenging circumstances for their lack of results**
- **Encouraging resilience among employees**
- **Dealing with a lack of ownership or accountability among employees for their results**

The survey identified lack of accountability as one of the top five sources of drama and causes of workplace emotional waste. In the next chapter, we'll take a deeper look at the ways ego gets in the way of accountability and how to bypass it to drive higher engagement and results.

6

UNDERSTANDING ACCOUNTABILITY

Accountability is the ultimate ego bypass. It defuses drama and eliminates emotional waste and, without question, is the true driver of results.

Like so many other things written about in this book, personal accountability is a choice. It's about taking responsibility for your actions and their consequences. For leaders, it's important to remember that accountability is not just a question of nature or nurture. Accountability can be developed.

Accountability is talked about a lot in organizations, but it's not well understood. Leaders get assigned the responsibility of "holding people accountable," and the subtext is about exerting power. Accountability gets "enforced" via policies, systems, and evaluations, and that tends to negatively affect engagement and motivation. My question is, How can you hold someone *else* accountable? Leaders have the right and responsibility to insist on accountability, but individuals ultimately decide whether to step up or not.

I believe that reality is the most motivating force for accountability. Leaders who constantly sugarcoat difficult issues or attempt to bend or soften reality are enabling others and protecting ego.

Accountability is about empowering oneself. When people don't see themselves as having the power to enforce accountability in others, they turn to leaders to do it for them. Focusing on reality is a better way to highlight and foster accountability. Let me give you an example from my own experience.

A physician I worked with had steadfastly refused to comply with a company initiative that I had been assigned to oversee. Physicians and nurses were told to proactively reach out to patients with chronic conditions and encourage them to show up for their preventive care clinic appointments. I explained the purpose of the initiative to this physician's nurse, emphasizing that providing excellent patient care was at its heart. But the physician had told his nurse the equivalent of "they are not the boss of us." The reach-out calls weren't happening.

That physician and nurse did not report to me. I had no "power" over them. But I was accountable for making the initiative work. As part of my responsibility, I had to report to the executive medical staff meeting on compliance. At one of these meetings, I reported out the compliance scores, which I had shown to the physician before my presentation. At the time, he said he was fine with it. My report focused only on data. I didn't tattle or try to get the physician in trouble. I just stuck with the facts.

Afterward, the physician and I connected. He asked, "Did you present that slide you showed me? Where was I on the compliance list?"

"You were last," I said.

But wait, he responded. Had I told the executive council that he had the highest number of patients at the clinic? And that they were the most chronic? Did I point out that he served on the most committees? I had made sure they understood how busy he was, right?

It was clear he had wanted me to do what others had done for him in the past, which was to embroider the data with his excuses. He had expected me to soften the reality that he was at zero compliance. My report showed who had complied with the initiative and who had not. The natural consequences flowed from there. I didn't need to wield power or be his boss. I just needed to deliver a dose of reality by not enabling or excusing his lack of accountability.

After that meeting, his nurse began making the calls.

Factors and Phases: Defining Accountability

My views about accountability are largely influenced by research I did a few years ago. We gave our accountability assessment to 1,500 people. Then we sorted the data into three groups to find the employees with the highest scores. We selected 200 people with high scores to participate in focus groups and asked them two questions: What is accountability to you? How did you become a person who is accountable?

Based on that research, we got a good definition for accountability along with how it gets established and strengthened. Four factors of accountability emerged in the feedback we gathered in the focus groups, along with five phases of development. We learned that accountability wasn't a skill set, it was a mind-set. It is about committing, without conditions, and staying the course.

Leaders have a key role to play in influencing and facilitating team members' choices to move to higher consciousness and ever-evolving states of accountability. We've used insights gleaned from the data to create tools and resources to help leaders do that.

FOUR FACTORS OF ACCOUNTABILITY
1. **Commitment**
2. **Resilience**
3. **Ownership**
4. **Continuous learning**

FIVE PHASES OF DEVELOPMENT
1. **Challenge**
2. **Experienced accountability**
3. **Feedback**
4. **Self-reflection**
5. **Collegial mentoring**

Breaking Down the Factors

Commitment

Let's start here, because lack of commitment should be a non-starter. If you have people withholding their commitment to making the company great, and you allow them to stay with the organization, that's insane. Think about it. Would you accept someone on an Olympic team if they weren't committed to doing whatever it took—training, eating right, total dedication—to turn in the best possible performance? Sometimes leaders notice unwillingness, but instead of directly asking for commitment, they pin their faith on hope.

Leaders assume commitment but fail to ask for it directly. They set expectations, assign projects, ask for deliverables, and then hope (fingers crossed!) that employees will step up. Highlight accountability by closing the deal. Ask questions that get at willingness: "What is your level of commitment? What is keeping you from being committed? What is your plan to get committed? Can I count on you to do this?" Explicitly asking for commitment is like getting informed consent. The verbal agreement becomes an informal contract.

It's what the airline attendants do when you're sitting in an exit row. They don't just assume you'll help out in the event of a plane crash. In fact, they know that without verbal, eye-to-eye consent, the passengers might be tempted to stay put and wait for someone else to act. Even when they're met with eye rolls and jokes, airline attendants insist that every person in the exit row says an out-loud "Yes" to committing to emergency procedures, which include opening the door and helping other passengers get to safety. A "No" means the person gives up the seat.

Resilience

Once you've established willingness and verified commitment, look for ways to help employees develop resiliency. Although you can only ask for commitment, you can help employees develop resiliency.

For example, we know that resiliency requires problem-solving skills. Leaders teach resiliency when they ask questions that help people self-reflect rather than jumping in themselves to solve problems. Good questions can inspire people to look for alternative answers, to find resources that they have not yet explored.

Resiliency is also about more than persistence, stamina, or stubbornness. Indeed, it has an element of collaboration and relationship building. People who are resilient are less likely to heroically forge ahead on their own. Instead, they reach out early and often to their networks, internally and externally, not looking for rescue but for suggestions on ways to move forward. They develop new networks when necessary. The most resilient people develop large networks marked by positive relationships, established partly by their own willingness to help others in times of need.

One way to help people get actively engaged in their own problem-solving is through something we call resiliency boards. The process is a great way to get unstuck when individuals or teams face a barrier and are stumped about how to clear the hurdle. It begins by coming up with a clear, direct question that frames the problem, then getting that question out to networks, known and unknown. People can put the question out in an email, in an online forum, in chat rooms, through social media— even post a flip chart in the break room. They're not asking anyone to completely solve the problem, just asking for suggestions on a next step, something to try, another person to contact, a resource they hadn't thought of.

After the suggestions are collected, the people or team use the list wholeheartedly, without cherry-picking items, and report back to colleagues about what was learned and which ideas paid off. This reinforces the learning and helps others expand their own learning and resiliency.

Ownership

This is where the "account" in accountability comes into play. How do people "own" their piece of whatever the results turn out to be? How do they see their role in impact and outcome? Ownership is basically the willingness to accept the consequences—whether positive or negative—of what happens. For those who are all in and wholehearted, ownership doesn't hurt. But it can be painful for the people who are half-hearted and hoping to keep that hidden.

People who take ownership are willing to dive deep and explore the specific actions that lead to the desired outcome. They take the time to account for their actions and reflect on the things they might do differently in the future. Ownership is shown through prolific use of the pronoun "I." You'll hear things like "I chose," "I denied," "I assumed," "I decided." Employees who speak in such ways can hear feedback without pain or defensiveness because they are eager to know how to develop in a way that helps them to be more effective. Defensiveness is a good sign that people are operating from ego instead of ownership. People who take ownership don't spin stories or generate drama. They are the ones who are hungry to find a new approach, a different tactic that would lead to better results. They want to know where to grow next. Ownership is the bedrock of accountability, and it sets the stage for evolution. It sets up conditions that allow leaders to identify the developmental needs that can be addressed to respond differently in the future. (See the tools for accountability in the appendix tool kit.)

Continuous Learning

This factor of accountability is commonly overlooked, but it's a way of life for those who are highly accountable. One of the reasons leaders are so frustrated today is that they have to work so hard holding people accountable. We've all seen the person who is perfectly willing to take responsibility for a mistake or failure but makes similar mistakes again and again. That shows an unwillingness to truly learn from mistakes, and if that's happening, game over.

It's a wonderful thing to make an account of and take ownership for results, but continual learners are those who can capitalize on their mistakes. They're willing to commit, with confidence, to different results with clarity around what will be required of them to do it.

Five Phases of Developing Accountability

To create a workforce that engages to create remarkable results, it is imperative to stop taking the pain away. Instead, support employees in a way that helps them deal with the random shocks that are bound to happen in today's economy.

Employees who are high in accountability succeed in spite of circumstances because they're resilient and committed and deal with the consequences of their actions.

Our questions to the high accountables led to a major breakthrough in understanding how leaders can intentionally create conditions that fuel the development of accountability. When asked how they themselves got to be high in accountability, the highly accountable respondents described what we divided into a five-phase process.

Challenge

If accountability is dropping in the workplace, it's likely because people are being underchallenged. Leaders have told me they're delegating less and less out of worry that employees' jobs are too big. They fret about overwhelming people by giving them too many challenges. But highly accountable people told us they don't need leaders to soften the message or protect them from difficult realities. Leaders just need to up the support. Delegation is a great way to encourage accountability development, especially with people who need to grow in the area you're assigning. The key is to have people's backs by providing feedback and mentoring—not by rescuing.

Work is commissioned based on the needs of the organization. The leader's responsibility here is to get help for the people who have gaps in their skills or competencies so they can step up and do what's required for growth and innovation. This is key to another phase of development.

Experienced Accountability

Leaders should resist the urge to protect people from natural consequences. It's not easy. It certainly wasn't easy for me to present a report without excusing the physician who refused to comply with the company initiative. But it's important not to interfere with the communication loop between reality and employees. People's choices, and the consequences that go with them, should be made visible and undiluted. You don't need to rescue people unless they are truly at risk or the greater good is threatened. Otherwise, let the chips land where they may, but be ready to shine a spotlight on where they landed. After an employee gets data from reality, leaders can be ready to jump in with the next phase of accountability development.

Feedback

The key focus for leaders is to inspire self-examination. You can do this through observation and stating the facts. Keep your discussions short and simple. Just communicate clearly about what you and others see. Often just a few sentences outlining what happened can be magical. Follow up with "Don't take my word for it, check it out for yourself by . . ." Then add an assignment to prompt self-reflection and set a date for a future conversation about what the employee discovered.

Use feedback to create a simple interruption of current thinking. If the feedback goes much beyond an observation of the facts, you're going to hook the ego. And the ego's main survival technique is defensiveness. Lose the long editorials and didactic speeches. Report what you see, but quickly turn over responsibility for improvement to the person to whom it belongs—the employee. That is what leads to another phase of accountability development.

Self-Reflection

This is absolutely the most important aspect of developing and sustaining accountability. I really hammer this point with leaders: "Feedback short. Self-reflection long." The ego's stories are a powerful impediment to personal development. The linchpin of accountability is a private, meditative state of inquiry that invites an unvarnished look at one's thinking and subsequent behavior. That's because self-reflection comes from a place of seeking truth, leading to an inner discovery rather than trying to force it through external pressure.

Leaders can fuel the self-reflection process with great questions and simple assignments. Journaling helps. Questions for self-reflection sound like these: What was your part in this outcome? What did you do that hindered results? What helped? What would great look like in this situation? What do you know for sure? What might you do to add value here?

Help employees see the stories that are getting in the way of their development. Ask: If you didn't have the story you're telling yourself right now, who would you be? What are you hoping to create? What is your goal? How is it working for you? What might happen if you changed your approach? The emphasis is always on the highest good and the actions people can take to ensure that.

An assignment might include asking people to connect with someone who is generally successful in similar situations and getting tips or suggestions on how to develop to obtain similar outcomes. In one case, I invited an employee whose body language and facial expressions were putting people off in meetings to record himself with an iPad. "Don't take my word for it. See what you notice after you record yourself." He was able to identify the ways his body language and methods of engaging were getting in the way of collaboration.

After giving people time to reflect, set a time to return to the conversation with a focus on what they noticed. Invite them to share the insights they gained from the contemplation. If you need to get even more concrete, give them assignments with deliverables to drive tougher self-reflection. Set up a time to reconnect and discuss the possibility of new commitments for action based on what they've learned about the situation and themselves. Employees explore their behavior and develop an expertise in self. Exercising the self-awareness muscle helps people see the situation more clearly, including their reactions and the choices for action in the face of reality. People learn to recognize when the ego, narrating in their heads, leads them astray, and they gain the ultimate freedom—the ability to stop believing everything they think.

If you think about events or feedback that were life-changing for you, they probably sprang from a period of being able to work through defensiveness and anger until you could see the truth and the ways your actions contributed to a difficult situation. Often that feedback came from a trusted colleague or friend, and that's why the next phase of accountability development is important.

Collegial Mentoring

People often avoid self-reflection and defend the ego by seeking out others to verify their invented stories. They'll track down coworkers or other leaders in an attempt to negate the dose of reality they have been provided. The ego is looking for rescue, and it seeks others to let it off the hook. In defense mode, people typically try three times to get someone to tell them that they don't see reality or don't agree with it, or to discredit the person who provides feedback. It is easy to fall into the trap of wanting to comfort or soften reality for that person, but when that happens, it only soothes the ego and aborts self-reflection. When accountability is hardwired into the system, collegial mentoring is absolutely essential. Good feedback comes from many sources—colleagues, customers, and vendors.

Leaders give feedback and assignments for self-reflection, and colleagues need to do their part to keep people there. They hold the space for it. Feedback can be given kindly, but the demand is to look fearlessly at reality and acknowledge what is true. Colleagues can disclose their own encouraging reactions to the feedback and insights they have gained by doing their own courageous acts of self-reflection. Adding concrete, factual observations is also a gentle way of saying "Hey, give the leader the benefit of the doubt in this situation."

When calls to greatness come from someone besides the leader, I call it "sense-making mentoring." Let me give you an example. If I give an employee some feedback about his role in a difficult situation, he may leave my office frustrated with me as a boss and convinced that I don't understand the situation or I have unrealistic expectations. This is where a collegial mentor gets to work. The worst thing that mentor can do is say "You poor thing. That does not sound fair. I think you are fabulous. This is not about you." What's more useful is to say "I would encourage you to take a look and find what fits from the feedback. What parts could be true?" or "I have known you for a few years, and this is what I see. When you worked for Ralph, it was all Ralph. And when you worked with Sue, she was the problem. Now you are working for Cy, and it's happening again. It seems like there is a theme there, which could provide a life lesson for you." This is a conversation from someone who is ready to help bypass the ego, help a colleague find a key lesson, and make a call to greatness.

Let me give you an example of how accountability development for an entire organization can look based on a client who was trying to resolve a literal life-and-death problem.

A Story of Accountability

For people who work hands-on with patients in a clinical environment, exposure to serious diseases happens every day. I'm talking about potentially horrific, life-threatening diseases here, the kind that inspire zombie movies. In these circumstances, you'd think that healthcare workers would clamor for all the protective equipment they could get their hands on.

It's a strange paradox of human behavior that when risk becomes routine, people often stop seeing danger. The constant exposure to health hazards leads to feelings of being invincible: "It could never happen to me." This was the situation at a large healthcare organization where I consulted.

The Occupational Health and Safety Administration (OSHA),

a federal agency, has mandated that caregivers wear protective clothing and equipment to shield them from diseases transmitted through bodily fluids, such as saliva, blood, and urine. The rules are intended for workers' safety and to help stop the spread of serious infectious diseases, such as HIV/AIDS and hepatitis C. Despite the mandates, many nurses at the region's healthcare centers considered safety eyewear a personal choice.

One senior leader, whom I'll call Michelle, was charged with fixing the problem, which was affecting her professionally and personally. She was heartsick over stories like that of the young nurse who, in her prime childbearing years, neglected to use the required eyewear and was exposed to HIV. Another nurse who hadn't used protective equipment contracted a staph infection, risking the health of her entire family. The consequences of exposure could have devastating consequences to a person's lifelong health.

Professionally, Michelle worried about the high costs associated with failure to adhere to mandated policies. When nurses were exposed, they couldn't work, which affected staffing. The incidents also escalated healthcare costs. And the patients themselves were also affected, because they had to undergo extra testing to assess for serious, contagious diseases. The employer is required to cover treatment as part of occupational hazard insurance.

In 2014, Michelle tackled the problem using all the conventional leadership techniques at her disposal. She formed a cross-functional team to come up with root causes for noncompliance and to develop additional policies and procedures to enforce compliance. She set about perfecting circumstances. When the team discovered that the eyewear was often ill-fitting and obstructed vision, the hospital acquired high-quality eyewear and lanyards. The glasses were made available at convenient places throughout nursing stations.

Feedback from employees also revealed an ego-based core belief that exposure wouldn't happen to them because they were "always careful." Michelle and her colleagues responded with an education and training campaign. They initiated a communication blitz with posters, emails, and meetings about OSHA rules. Performance management policies were updated and disciplinary actions were taken, including the possibility of termination for violating the protective eyewear policy. Leaders begged, pleaded, held contests, and rewarded people for doing something that should have been nonnegotiable.

After all that hard work, they were able to reduce exposure by a small percentage but hadn't achieved the goal of full compliance. Leaders were tired. The nurses felt hassled and irritated. And as soon as leaders let up on the policing, exposure rates crept up. What they were doing wasn't self-sustaining.

Michelle was beyond frustrated. She had tapped into all the conventional wisdom and best practices she was aware of, expecting great results. But they'd barely made a dent in the compliance rates.

A New Way of Seeing

After getting training in Reality-Based philosophies and tools, Michelle decided to take a new approach. She recognized that she had to stop apologizing for having high standards around exposure and that the organization had to make wearing eyewear a nonnegotiable practice.

After leaders ensured that everyone had proper eyewear, managers were asked to meet with employees individually and ask about their commitment to using the eyewear. If an employee expressed unwillingness, the next question was "What is your plan for becoming willing?"

When exposures happened, leaders asked employees to account for the choices they made around not keeping their commitment to safety. Those who chose not to don the eyewear, endangering themselves and others, were disciplined or even terminated. Patient care units that achieved zero exposures were rewarded.

The questions at meetings changed from "why we can't" get zero exposure rates to "how we can." Discussions centered on what true commitment looked like. Patient care was brought to the forefront—patients were there to be healed, not further harmed.

Leaders implemented just-in-time questions to bypass ego and spur self-reflection: Why would you choose to risk your life rather than be safe? What can we do as a team to change this situation? What is something you, as an individual, could do to make a difference? How can you help?

Leaders moved the focus from inventing processes and mandating compliance to insisting on personal accountability and shared responsibility. They stopped "group coaching" through awareness campaigns and replaced it with personal coaching focused on giving individual nurses good mental processes that hardwired accountability. Exposure rates have moved down steadily, and the resistance to the eyewear has faded. Today you see people donning the glasses and offering eyewear to others who forget. Safety has become the norm. Michelle has been able to share with other healthcare safety leaders in the region her success and the process for achieving it.

> **According to the Reality-Based Leadership/ Futures Study, convincing people to try new things and overcoming resistance to change consumed 13 percent of leaders' time, time that was squandered on emotional waste.**

One thing our research and experience has helped us know for sure: Today's accountability drives tomorrow's results. An investment in developing accountability will reap the biggest payoff you can imagine.

7

CHANGE MANAGEMENT IS SO
20TH CENTURY

It was 1989 when I gave my first presentation to a national organization of leaders on the importance of recognizing and being ready for change. The key message was "change is coming, we can't stop it, and we've got to get good at it." My presentation included insights and tools and was full of forward-thinking tactics to get employee buy-in, lead employees through emotional transitions, and lock in new behaviors. It was a new, timely topic with a timely, game-changing message for the eager leaders of 1989.

I stayed to listen to the presentation after mine and was glad I did. It featured an unconventional message on the critical importance of developing keyboarding skills because everyone would soon be working on desktop computers. That message sounded so innovative that, as a leader in my organization, I quickly fell in line with my Human Resource leader's recommendation that we administer keyboarding fluency tests to every job applicant at our organization.

By now, many of you have experienced this puzzling step in the job application process. Many organizations continue to assess office and software fluency as a nonnegotiable competency for hiring. And yet we don't require that people come into our organizations with the agility and resiliency skills that are essential to deal with change. Today, individuals who lack computer skills have extremely limited employment options, while an inability to anticipate and respond well to change isn't necessarily considered an obstacle.

Why "Change Management" Needs to Die

Today, it would be laughable to have a presentation on the necessity of keyboarding skills. Yet after 30 years of organizations and academics studying the practice of change management, the same tired change management conversations soldier on. Organizations are doing little to insist that people get themselves proficient at change.

Thirty years of change management studies have been published; policies and training have proliferated. Myriad books have been written. Energy, time, and money have been poured into leadership philosophies centering on change management. HR and external influencers have hammered leaders about the importance of "managing change."

I should know. For a long time, I was one of them.

Conventional wisdom is what's currently provided to leaders in many leadership development programs and Human Resources curricula. And it doesn't work. It might have been cutting-edge thinking 30 years ago, but now it's the equivalent of using a typewriter when we can use our thumbs to text or voice dictation that is transcribed in real time by apps. Today we have virtual reality, holograms, and robots.

It's time to blow up the myths embedded in change management philosophies. Consider this: Much of the change management training I see actively circling in HR and leadership training is founded on theories and research conducted decades ago, even before desktop computers were commonplace. Here are the three I see most frequently:

1948—Kurt Lewin describes three states of change—unfreezing, moving, and refreezing. Lewin was a social psychologist whose innovative research uncovered group dynamics and the influence of the status quo in a wartime era (World War II). This was before computers, before short job tenure became the norm, and at a time when the workforce was primarily a male-dominated manufacturing environment.

1979—William Bridges, a speaker, author, and consultant, uses a change model of transition as ending, neutral zone, and new beginning. Unlike earlier models that speak of institutionalizing or "freezing" behaviors, Bridges's attention is focused on helping people discover, accept, and embrace their new identities in the new situation. His approach is meant to lead to major psychological changes, and he often spoke of using the model to cope with the death of his wife.

1996—John Kotter launches his eight-step change model via Harvard Business School. It was communicated as eight common failure points that

Kotter observed in large organizations over the course of the 1980s. These failure points were still grounded in the late 1980s and early 1990s, long before computers or even dial-up AOL were common in the workplace. Kotter's work was an excellent call to creating awareness of what can be messy new business initiatives, not permanent change readiness.

I am amazed that change management continues to be one of most requested topics from Reality-Based Leadership. Organizations still use this outdated philosophy as they struggle with how to keep people primed for the fast and furious changes spurred by a global marketplace. Let's face it. Fast and furious is about the only flavor change comes in, and that is about the only thing that isn't going to change. Keeping people curious and competent is an organizational imperative. Companies need to be able to count on people who are resilient. They need to work with the willing, people ready to do what it takes to drive results. Change management is not going to get them there. In today's organizations, there needs to be a key mind-set shift. To be relevant in the future, leaders need to leave change management theories in the past and focus instead on readiness, or the development of an employee's future potential. In my previous two books, I introduced a new metric to measure employee value:

Current Performance
(How am I doing today?)
+
Future Potential
(How am I preparing for what's next?)
−
(3x) Emotional Expense
(Amount of emotional waste and drama)

= EMPLOYEE VALUE

Capitalizing on change is about maximizing future potential, right? By developing the necessary job fluency skills long before they're needed, organizations can hone the competency of capitalizing on change, which provides a far stronger competitive advantage than managing change. Old theories of change management designed to help people cope with change leaves leaders overmanaging, overcoddling, and underleading. They fail to call employees to step up, be fluent in the now, and be ready for what is next.

Change and Emotional Waste

As students of common conventional wisdom, many leaders probably have been taught to spend hours massaging the message to defuse arguments and get buy-in to key strategic initiatives. Perhaps you've felt compelled to apologize for all the change that constantly rocks your organization. You've spent hours perfecting a process to approach, communicate, and reinforce the new process, project, or work situation.

In my work, I find smart and successful leaders approaching change with trepidation and kid gloves, hoping to avoid the pain of inflicting another change on employees. With their engagement scores hanging in the balance, they've nodded in sympathy and overcoddled when employees say they need time to grieve before they can commit to strategic business decisions.

NO EGO CORE BELIEF
Attachment is the source of suffering. Get
fluent in the new but not attached.

If you or the leaders in your organization fit this description, you've just diagnosed a key source of emotional waste. I'll be showing you a way to take back your time as a leader and cultivate employee readiness to capitalize on change.

Resistance to change, which is exacerbated by the traditional change management philosophies, is among the top five generators of drama and emotional waste, according to our Reality-Based Leadership/Futures Survey. Developing new mind-sets and leadership competencies will help you drastically reduce this source of emotional waste. Abandoning change management and focusing on business readiness gets people fluent in the now and ready for what's next. Business readiness is vital to creating and sustaining great results.

Our pain is not from the changes in our lives but from our resistance to those changes.

Enter Bold New Thinking

In my experience, people respond to change in one of two ways. The first is with a sense of excitement and eagerness to capitalize on the possibilities change can bring. People roll up their sleeves, dig into what is new and different, and figure out how to make changes that move the organization forward.

The second way, in the face of the exact same circumstances, is to erect a wall of resistance. People spend precious work hours expressing their shock, their surprise, their dismay. They complain about the direction their companies are taking. They question the competency of the leader who made the decision and the intelligence of those who agree with it. They blame others for their lack of action, driving their BMWs (bitching, moaning, and whining) over to anyone who will sympathize about the horrors of change. They begin a spiral down into doubting their own survival abilities.

In other words, they generate enormous drama and emotional waste. They pine for the past and demand that leaders bend reality to keep their worlds from changing.

The drag of resistance to change and emotional waste are exacerbated by myths embedded in outdated change management approaches. These myths stay alive as long as leaders use them to sympathize with and coddle employees. To obliterate these myths, I issue a new call to greatness for readiness, which can be achieved by debunking the myths we've been clinging to about change management. By removing the limiting beliefs the myths are based on, we can move from resistance into readiness.

Myth #1: Change Is Hard

Leaders who believe that change is hard tend to overmanage and underlead. They develop and employ methods that stunt people's growth and set the table for habitual resistance. Efforts designed to take the suffering out of change, however well-intentioned, are based on the faulty assumption that change causes suffering. By attempting to remove the discomfort that comes with learning something new, leaders don their hero suits to protect their teams and coddle employees, which contributes to a passive attitude about preparing for the future and doesn't allow people to experience the gift reality gives us—circumstances that require new skills to adapt and progress. There's a well-tested theory for this, and it's called evolution. Species that tend to advance are those that are not protected. They are best suited to adapt to new and changing circumstances. Coddled employees see imperfect circumstances and their personal pain as an excuse not to perform. They are constantly taken by surprise when change happens and view taking action as optional. They choose suffering over succeeding.

If the goal is to make change manageable or easier to bear, leaders typically become the ones who shoulder the burden. They must create an inspired vision statement. They are the ones investing great energy and resources in developing a perfect roll-out process. They spend hours crafting the ideal communication matrix. And by doing this, they reinforce a culture of learned helplessness. Way too many people see managing change as the leaders' responsibility. When employees figure change isn't their own responsibility, they fail to develop the resilience and skills to be ready for what is next.

Change is hard? Our research shows something different. Change is hard *only for the unready*. Change is painful only for people who attach their identities and happiness to a mythical perfect set of circumstances.

Let me give you an example. Say I have two employees, and I give each the latest, greatest smartphone. Its cutting-edge technology will help them be more effective at work.

Employee One has never skipped a software upgrade and prides herself on being technically savvy. She is familiar with all the apps that help her work more efficiently. When I hand her the new smartphone, she is super excited. Not only will this new phone give her an added edge at work, but she also can use it with a short learning curve. She is grateful that the organization she works for is on top of the latest technology. Because she works for that kind of organization, she feels extra engaged and is willing to go the extra mile.

Employee Two has never experienced a software upgrade because he's insisted on using the old flip phone he's had for years. In the past, he has complained that new technology is too hard to learn. He's bragged that he doesn't need all those newfangled apps to talk on the phone. When I make it clear that using a smartphone is now a condition of employment, Employee Two is overwhelmed by the unfamiliar technology and resentful that learning to use it takes so much time out of his day. He subjects his coworkers to a litany of complaints, and he constantly interrupts their work with questions about how the smartphone works. Because he skipped the upgrades, he isn't ready for what's next.

What is the variable here? It's not the phone. The phone is just a thing, a technology, a tool for getting work done. The change represented by the smartphone is neutral. Two employees got identical phones. The variable is the individual's change readiness. This leads us to the second myth about change.

> Change management is focused on making change least disruptive for employees. Business readiness is focused on making change least disruptive to businesses.

Myth #2: People Need Time to Grieve Change

When I hear people at work moaning about needing time to grieve a change, I immediately wonder, "Which beloved family member did they lose? Was their pet killed by a car?" In those scenarios, mourning would make total sense. I would insist they take time off to grieve with their loved ones.

Some of this workplace grief attitude springs from the work of Elizabeth Kübler-Ross, who identified five stages of grief: denial, anger, bargaining, depression, and acceptance. Her work centered on death and the dying, but it's been used in the workplace as a way to manage the "trauma" and suffering caused by change. Although change indeed can be a challenge, I don't see how it makes sense to grieve the natural and inevitable changes required to keep a business successful and sustainable in the same way as we would a death.

Seriously, do you really need time to grieve because you got new software? Because the needs of the business require that a project be eliminated? Because you have been assigned to work at a different desk? Or because a new organizational structure means you will be working with a new team?

The reality is, most of the changes we experience at work are about everyday improvements we need to make to adapt to a changing marketplace or work environment. Those kinds of changes are about maintaining a sense of readiness to stay relevant and competitive. They don't require grief counseling. That perspective is a major distraction to work that needs to be done to produce great results. In fact, employee evaluations, if you keep them at all, should be centered not on past performance but on readiness for the future.

Employees who are in a high state of readiness don't require time to grieve. They are aware, they are willing, they are advocates, and they are all in. These employees adjust their sails and chart a new course. They're not attached to the past because they're ready for the future. They're not naive about the realities of making change work, nor are they blind to the obstacles and difficulties of new processes or projects. But they're not generating emotional waste by arguing with reality. They're too busy ensuring a successful outcome and adding value because they were ready for what's next.

While working with a multinational pharmaceutical company,

I saw a great opportunity to gather data on my business readiness hypothesis. The company had long worked in a traditional, hierarchical office-and-cubicle environment. Senior leaders made a strategic decision to move to an open environment to foster more collaboration, cooperation, and creativity. Designated rooms still would be available for meetings or private conversations as needed, but, in general, the walls were coming down. Employee chatter about the impending change spanned the emotional spectrum, from predictions of doom to skepticism about the viability of the plan, from tentative exploration to excitement.

To see if readiness was linked to difficulty of change, we created a survey that would help us assess employees' state of readiness. Before the move, we asked questions to see how technology-savvy employees were. We inquired about the size of their networks, what current communication methods they used, whether they were up on new music, what innovative ways of working they had tried. How up-to-date were they on the news in their industry? Were they citizens of the modern world or still living in the past?

Three months after these folks moved into their new environment, we did another survey asking them to rate how hard the change was and how the company had managed it. We found an overwhelming correlation between people who were low in readiness and those who categorized the change as difficult. The employees who said they had really struggled with the open environment also were the most critical of the way the business managed the change. They stepped down into blame instead of stepping up to accountability.

Myth #3: We Can't Handle So Much Change

The marketplace will always be charging ahead. It's indifferent to whether people are uncomfortable, disturbed, or discombobulated.

Resistance comes from people who are fearful of being exposed as unready. It's an ego-driven response that motivates people to go to great lengths to avoid disruption. For the ego, change is like standing in an earthquake. It just yearns for the ground to stop shaking. "I don't like this, make it stop, why is this happening to me?" yells Ego. But you can't control an earthquake, you can only respond.

Sympathizing with the ego—coming to the rescue of people who resist—will result in a workforce that is fluent in the past. Sympathy reinforces the false premise that too much change, or any change at all, is painful and unmanageable. Complaints about too big or too much are a leadership legacy of coddling instead of preparing, and it doesn't serve people when leaders protect them. Instead of asking "How can we make this change easier for you?" leaders should be asking "How can we build your skills to make you better at change?" Managing to personal preferences or comfort levels stunts people's growth. It creates a pipeline of emotional waste, with money and time flowing down the drain.

Another common mistake in organizations is to turn everything into a formal major change initiative. The kinds of disruptions that require roll-out road maps and communication schemes often happen because people weren't paying attention to the big picture in the first place.

It doesn't have to be that way if change is managed incremental, digestible adjustments. Effective leaders he people understand that change is inevitable, necessary, and neutral. They coach people through the small, digestible downloads that create a workforce ready for what's next. They don't shield people from the growth that today's reality requires; they invest energy in helping them keep up with the times and hone their ability to be ready, willing, and able.

Substituting "daily leadership" for "change management" preempts the drama that generates emotional waste. No longer does the leader bear the burden of making change less disruptive and more comfortable. In such an environment, the major change initiative is reserved for the widespread, big-scope, major breakthrough events that spring from disruptive cultural or technological trends.

Myth # 4: We Can Control the Pace of Change

I travel a lot for my work. I have been to places that have odd pockets of high unemployment, yet often the employers I work with in these communities insist they can't find good people to hire for vital positions. How is it possible that high unemployment and inability to make good hires coexist? Jobs are available. What's missing is that people haven't made themselves ready for the jobs that exist. People have skipped the upgrades.

People who see change as an inside job see themselves as victims. They see change as something that is being done to them. But change is coming because of forces from the outside. Businesses don't have the luxury of slowing down change because their employees prefer it. If they want to stay competitive, they have to stop worrying about whether their employees are comfortable with the pace of change and drive their development in a way that gives them the abilities they need to make change work for the business. Keep reading. We can show you how.

8

BUSINESS READINESS

Business readiness isn't even a close relative to change management. It's a fresh, radical approach. It requires leaders to constantly deliver reality to people. They do it with transparency, direction, clear expectations—and without apology. Business readiness involves working diligently to enlist and direct people's energy into delivering great results no matter what the new reality is. Make the call to greatness.

Change management philosophy, rooted in passivity and transaction, has outlived whatever usefulness it ever had. Business readiness is the way to develop employees to have the agility and abilities to capitalize on change no matter what form it takes—marketplace disruptions, reorganizations, increased expectations, or changing needs of customers.

Business readiness disrupts the change management cycle of leaders doing the heavy lifting while employees vent and resist, which creates massive emotional waste. Traditional change management is about minimizing disruption for people. Business readiness ensures that change isn't disruptive to the

---

BUSINESS READINESS   131

business. Employees who are focused on business readiness step up willingness, participation, and shared responsibility for anticipating and responding to change.

Ego hates change, but it gets bypassed when leaders focus on what is best for the business rather than on self-interest or team preservation. Employees let go of their expectations to be led through change and step up eagerly to meet it or even find it. They take responsibility for sustaining their state of readiness so that their expertise and efforts are constantly directed to the future instead of clinging to the past.

Although business readiness begins in the same way as change management—with awareness—the paths quickly diverge. Leaders can't stop at awareness. They have to get directly involved in the things that will help employees take accountability for moving the business upward and onward through readiness.

Transparency is a keystone to high-functioning businesses. In an environment of business readiness, leaders share business information quickly and fluidly, without sugarcoating or softening reality. "Here is what we know today. Here is where you come in. How can you help?" This attitude moves people from passivity and resistance to accountable action. It's the difference between the questions "Is it necessary? Do we have to? Can we do this?" and "How will we do this? When can we start?" Leaders play a key role in directing employees toward vigorous purpose.

We use a pyramid to help people see the evolution of leading employees from awareness to become the ultimate drivers of change. The mind-set is a perpetual "What's next?" and the leader responds by helping people willingly step up to the next level.

Business Readiness Pyramid

Driver

Active Participant

Advocacy

Willing

Aware

Aware

Change management begins with awareness, but a business readiness mind-set changes the focus and goals. Building awareness is a transparent and interactive act. Rather than a one-way communication pipeline that feeds the ego and inspires resistance, it is accompanied by a call to greatness.

On the Business Readiness Pyramid, the idea is to quickly move employees from awareness of the change that is required to understanding the shared responsibility for making it happen. Once the business case has been made crystal clear, leaders can quickly get to: "How do you intend to step up and help get this done?"

Here's an example of why this second step in the awareness level is so crucial. One company I worked with was in the throes of change that was being throttled by employees who complained they were in the dark about strategic direction. Leaders were being emotionally blackmailed into thinking that inaction was the result of their failure to communicate. We kept hearing employees say "We don't know what is going on here. We don't understand the strategy or where it's taking us." One day, just before I went into a meeting to give a presentation, I stopped to use the bathroom. The strategic plan was posted at eye level on the inside door. There was no way to not see it.

As I began my presentation, I asked what kind of challenges people were facing. Imagine my surprise when the immediate feedback was about lack of communication. Employees said they didn't understand where the company was going or what it meant for them. I am not sure what exactly they were waiting for, but the expectation that they should be spoon-fed information was a form of resistance and a big cause of emotional waste. Information was everywhere—even in the bathroom! The employees weren't doing their part, which was to consume the information and figure out what was required of them to respond to the changes. Their egos were stuck in preference, so they chose dramatic opposition over adaptation.

Leaders play a pivotal role in moving people from awareness to willingness. It's important to move quickly from information to interaction by asking questions that bypass ego by inspiring self-reflection. The idea is to get to a stated commitment from employees.

Willing

With a focus on value-added adaptation and capitalizing on opportunity, leaders need to ask self-reflective questions like these: "Now that you know what is changing and are clear on the ways you are responsible for adapting, can I count on you? What is your level of willingness to step up? Can you say yes to what's next?" This gets leaders out of the dangerous territory of assuming.

Get specific. Ask people: "On a scale from 1 to 10, what is your level of commitment? Can I count on you?" If willingness is low, the next question for self-reflection is "What is your plan to get (more) willing?"

Too often, this conversation either doesn't happen, or it gets glossed over in a group setting. Willingness is frequently assumed even in the face of resistance. People often stay silent in meetings, then unload in meetings after the meetings. That's why willingness needs to be addressed with individuals by continually asking "Can I count on you? What is your plan to get on board?" and other questions that make willingness conscious and visible.

I am a firm believer that working with the willing gets you much further, much faster, than trying to coax aware-but-resistant people to get on board with a change. And once you ask for willingness, beware of sending mixed message by giving the unwilling time and attention. I write books on this and still screw it up (but only daily). Let me tell you a story about that.

Our family lives on a lake in Nebraska, and we love the water. Our boat is the last to leave its dock in the fall and the first to go into the lake at the earliest hint of spring. On any given weekend when the weather cooperates, I yell out morning orders: "Whoever wants to go out on the boat has 15 minutes to suit up and report to the dock." The boys know the drill, and they rush to get ready, putting on wetsuits to protect themselves from the early season's chilly water. Once they report to the dock, it's imperative to get them quickly into the lake. If they're waiting around in the sun with their wetsuits on, I'm going to have roasted sons.

One Saturday, I had several boys on the boat, suited up, ready, and willing to go. Me? I was in the kitchen, being an ineffective leader.

"Are you coming with us?" I asked Son Number Three. He was aware that his brothers were ready, willing, and waiting, but he was holding out, looking to craft the best deal for himself. He had demands: What if his friend called with something more fun to do? Would I turn the boat around and return him to the dock? Could we get good Subway sandwiches for lunch? Would I make the other boys listen to his music playlist? Could he be the first to wakeboard?

While I was in the kitchen negotiating with my little terrorist, the ready and the willing were on the boat, roasting. Their initial enthusiasm was converting to impatience and irritation. Why was the majority being held hostage to the one person who wanted his demands met before he'd get on board?

In organizations, once you have identified and activated the willing, stop trying to coax those who aren't. They'll either figure it out and jump in, or they won't and will miss the boat. Coaching conversations can make clear that full commitment and accountability are needed for the privilege of staying with the organization.

Advocacy

Once people have expressed willingness, it's time to up the ante. Most people will pledge commitment privately but can be reluctant to play publicly. Allowing a vocal minority to dominate conversations and group interactions is a derailing force. If you're like me, you've sat in innumerable meetings as leaders banged their heads against the wall of negativity constructed by vocal resisters, only to be bombarded with supportive comments, emails, and texts afterward. Not helpful. When it happens to me, I express gratitude for the support and point out how powerful it would have been to hear it in the room, in the moment.

The call for greatness here is about integrity. If you have pledged willingness and commitment, then make that visible through your public advocacy. Doing this will weed out the pretenders. If they can't bring themselves to be public advocates, they're still in ego mode. To counteract this, I recommend and teach an ego-bypass strategy called activating the silent majority.

I worked in one high-tech company that was very proud of its open, inclusive culture. Anyone could express an opinion about anything in the organization. This cultural norm was supported through an internal online chat forum. The intention was solid. In this open-source environment, everyone could chime in with their great ideas, collaborate on problems, and share information that brought the best ideas to the top. But the intention failed to live up to its promise when the channel was taken over by a vocal minority with strong opinions. They used the forum as a literal bully pulpit to question directions and decisions. They weren't offering expertise or helping to make things great, they were actively badmouthing and making the case for "why we can't" and "why we shouldn't."

Many colleagues privately expressed their frustration with this vocal minority. They were annoyed and put off by the nonstop criticism cloaked as "input" or their "rights" as employees. But because the majority remained mostly silent in the face of the naysayers, the impression was created that the vocal minority's views were mainstream and supported by others.

Leaders talked about shutting down the vocal minority, but I offered a different strategy: Activate your silent majority instead. How? For starters, when employees complained about the complainers, ask how they were using their own power. How were they asserting their inherent clout by logging in to refute the negativity? Were they standing up in meetings and publicly advocating for what they'd privately vowed to support?

Once leaders started coaching the silent majority to step up, people began chiming in, meeting the resisters in meetings and the chat room with arguments based on the company's business case. The silent majority no longer hid their support; they shook it out and wore it. Through advocacy, the online tool eventually was cleaned up by the no-longer-silent majority, and it returned to its original purpose. The chat room drama fizzled as ideas, creativity, and collegiality created a lively buzz that served the business. Once leaders and others stopped feeding the resistance through both attention and silence, advocacy ramped up and the resisters were exposed for who they were—a vocal minority.

Leaders can move people from passive silence to active advocacy by identifying low-drama individuals who tend to say yes. They can create a picture of what visible, verbal advocacy looks like and ask questions for self-reflection: "Can I count on you to speak up early and often in the next company town hall meeting in support of this topic?" or "Can I count on you to reframe a negative hallway conversation by highlighting the potential this project has for the company's future?" Leaders can help employees create an elevator speech based on the business case so they are rehearsed in on-the-spot advocacy wherever the need arises—in the elevator, the bathroom, the break room.

After facilitating awareness, willingness, and advocacy, leaders are ready to harness the energy of active participation. From a state of higher consciousness, the call to action becomes a shared responsibility to adapt the work, the teams, and the structures to support new realities, to drive results, and to sustain a constant state of readiness.

Active Participant

With a barrier-free mental state, the willing advocates step up into right action. The leader's call to greatness is directed toward creating excellent results by integrating the new reality into the day-to-day work.

As the leader communicates the changes required, the employees become active participants by incorporating that information and offering up the ways they can adjust and align with the new direction. They help each other deliver their work in new, more effective ways. Shared responsibility requires self-reflection as opposed to reaction. The leader sets the expectation that employees will move beyond personal preference to deliver on the potential embedded in the business case for change.

Creating clear charters and explaining explicit deliverables are the leader's role here, using the tools offered in this book that will help people bypass the ego. Employees become partners in change and the architects of their responses to the new reality. They no longer see themselves as victims; now they actively capitalize on the opportunities the change presents. They take responsibility for building the skills and competencies they need to be fluent in now and are ready for what's next.

Leaders have a role here, again, with questions for self-reflection: "What is your plan for adapting? How are you going to structure your work to deliver what is required? What do you think is required of you to make this change? How will you meet that requirement?"

Shellie, a director in a consulting company that provides predictive analytics and labor management services, is trained in Reality-Based methods. Her company was initiating several projects to respond to an increasingly complex marketplace that put new demands on the business. One day, in a textbook Open-Door Policy session, an unhappy employee drove his BMW to her office to vent about his lack of opportunity in the new plans and his fear of being left out. He saw colleagues on his team getting assigned to work on high-profile projects and change initiatives, and he felt sidelined. He accused Shellie of playing favorites.

Shellie's training helped her resist getting hooked by his complaint. Instead of responding with blame or defensiveness, she asked: "What is stopping you from raising your hand?"

There were abundant challenging projects to tackle, she pointed out. Other team members had actively stepped up and offered their energy and talents to move the initiatives forward. Shellie asked the employee: "What projects and actions are you willing to commit to that would help move these projects along?" This helped bypass the employee's ego, and he began to see the story he had created for himself. Others weren't "provided" opportunities. He had failed to raise his hand and actively campaign for involvement. Although he was willing, he had passively waited for someone to hand him a plum assignment.

The director reviewed a list of important projects. "What are you willing to volunteer for?" She committed to match his level of commitment and enthusiasm with her support and encouragement. Instead of the emotional waste that a venting conversation normally produces, Shellie's questions were a catalyst for the employee to edit his story and make different choices. He redirected his energy from drama to productivity, boosting his performance and elevating team productivity and results.

When leaders help employees bypass ego, it allows employees to see how their stories prevent them from capitalizing on opportunities and reaping the rewards of full participation. In active participation, employees report to work ready. They're not confused, needy, resistant, or passively waiting for the leader to tell them what to do. They're excited about the possibilities, working to figure out what they know, what they don't know, and how to fill in the gaps.

And now leaders can take them to the top of the pyramid, that one last call to greatness. Such leaders facilitate employees becoming drivers.

Driver

In an organization, it isn't efficient for leaders to be the main drivers of change. Employees are the ones closest to the marketplace, and they can be invaluable resources for helping the organization know what's next. Drivers aren't waiting for the leader to tell them; they're on top of the situation. Drivers constantly scan the horizon. They're the scouts. Drivers become the internal disruptors—the preemptive, innovative thought leaders.

That's what a leader wants, but it is important to proceed with caution. You don't want people driving without a license. They have to prove they're ready. They have to have evolved through the pyramid of awareness, willingness, advocacy, and active participation. They need to be aligned with the organization and grounded in reality. It's important not to feed egos by acquiescing to hostile requests to drive from people who fancy themselves as enlightened and capable but who haven't logged in the hours on the road. You want drivers who are credible and trusted. People who want to be in control by offering opinions but not expertise will slow things down, maybe even slam on the brakes. The license to drive comes through demonstrated delivery in the now, a solid grasp of reality, and preparedness for what's next.

True drivers talk about how to make change work and how it will work, with a constant gaze to the future. Even the best performers and technical geniuses risk becoming irrelevant if they're not constantly scanning the horizon for potential bumps in the road and trends coming down the pike. They don't just spot them; they act by innovating and removing barriers.

Assessing for Readiness

Business readiness is so vital to success that I would champion the idea of making it a bold new metric that replaces performance evaluation. Performance evaluation is about what happened in the past. Business readiness is the key indicator of how employees and the organization will deliver value and results far into the future. Leaders can develop measurements based on pyramid elements for the individual, the team, and the organization. Assess people's awareness of industry trends, strategic focus, and levels of preparing for what's next. Measure employees' willingness and alignment. And finally, advocacy—how activated is the silent majority? How many people are participating on teams, projects, restructuring? What kinds of ideas are coming from the active participants? Are their recommendations based on best practices and innovation? Or are folks making only incremental changes or still trying to preserve what was? How much emotional waste is being created or reduced? Setting the expectation for business readiness and then measuring it creates an organizational call to greatness.

One group that nailed it? The Nebraska Medical Center, a client we have been working with for many years, which has the largest biocontainment unit in the country.

Ten years before such units played a crucial role in preventing national health disasters, a talented team of healthcare professionals was looking for the "what's next." They saw the value in creating and maintaining readiness for disasters so they could instantly and effectively respond to plane crashes, multivictim trauma such as shootings, nuclear accidents, and the like. Establishing a high level of disaster preparedness would help the medical center better serve those it was committed to serving and give the center an edge in the marketplace. This team, operating high on the pyramid, became active participants in planning and executing drills for preparedness and in educating others.

As drivers, this highly functioning team looked to the future and saw another health threat that wasn't being addressed. In a global marketplace that allows for fast, efficient travel throughout the world, a highly infectious, deadly disease— think Ebola virus—can spread like a raging wildfire no matter where it originates. The current state was that many healthcare workers weren't even willing, much less trained, to care for the people who got such diseases. And unless an infection was treated and contained quickly, there was a real risk of an epidemic that could devastate the medical community and surrounding populations.

The team mobilized, garnering the resources that would allow members to build a biocontainment unit with a highly skilled staff. These medical professionals weren't pie-in-the-sky doomsayers. They were visionaries who were grounded in reality and knowledge, expertise and innovation. They saw what was coming, what was needed, and stepped up.

And that day came. Ebola erupted in Africa and eventually arrived in the United States.

Nebraska Medicine was ready. The medical staff not only treated Ebola patients but saved their lives and mitigated the threat of nationwide contagion. Staff members were in a state of readiness for patients who needed the best of our healthcare system. Because Nebraska Medicine had focused on business readiness, those patients got the best. They survived, and a serious healthcare crisis was averted.

In the aftermath of the Ebola crisis, Nebraska Medicine was in a unique position to capitalize on the opportunities created by its response to the crisis. The center became a partner with the federal government to create nationwide systems to address new threats. The staff became key players in helping other healthcare organizations to build their capacities to be ready for what's next. Now Nebraska Medicine leads the nation in readiness efforts and has received millions of dollars in grants and other funding to continue to innovate and educate others. Business readiness put the center in a position to capitalize on the opportunity and to secure major funding for its efforts—not an easy feat in health care today.

Although the day-to-day issues of most companies might not involve these kinds of dramatic life-and-death issues, this example shows what is possible when organizations shift focus from change management to business readiness.

9

BUY-IN

As leaders, how many of your conversations revolve around trying to get the proverbial buy-in?

How do we get buy-in?

Do we have buy-in?

I think we lack buy-in.

What will it take to get buy-in?

Next time you find yourself engaging in one of these common conversations, just imagine the sound of emotional waste as it circles the drain.

Telling leaders that it's their responsibility to get buy-in is another piece of failed conventional wisdom. Not only does it give leaders an impossible burden, but it assigns a passive role to the person to whom buy-in belongs. Leaders who solicit buy-in allow change-resistant people to hold the organization hostage. These leaders spin their wheels and tap dance frantically, trying to get something that should be nonnegotiable.

> Fourteen percent of the time that leaders said they were dealing with drama on their teams involved working with their teams to get buy-in:
> - Dealing with employees who withheld buy-in to organizational strategies
> - Managing poor employee attitudes about things that couldn't be changed or were nonnegotiable
> - Handling employees who were upset about not being consulted before decisions were made

When leaders are assigned to get buy-in, what follows is like an episode of *Mission Impossible*. They can't manufacture, purchase, assign, or demand buy-in, though lord knows they try. They produce a pitch for the perfect plan, try to impress people with an impeccable idea, or create ways to convince others that the change is compelling. Instead of leading, they become naggers in chief, spending fruitless time arguing or cajoling. It's another form of coddling.

In business, buy-in is not an option that can be ordered up like leather seats on a car or a playroom in a house. It's a condition of employment, a core job responsibility. It is the way people are supposed to show up. Instead of making it clear that buy-in is a requirement, leaders falsely believe they must work to deserve it, and they exhaust themselves trying to create impossibly perfect circumstances to earn it.

No amount of money allows leaders to purchase buy-in, and they should stop trying to do so. Every time they try, they are indulging the ego, building entitlement, and reinforcing victim mind-sets.

I always recommend that leaders work with the willing. Buy-in means "I am willing." Like accountability and engagement, it's a choice. It's a declaration of commitment and the first step toward action. The leader's role is to discover those who have chosen to buy in and then to work with the willing to create great results.

The role of leaders is to help people get clear on the fact that if they want to play on the team, buy-in is a prerequisite. Coaching that inspires self-reflection is a great way to be up front and clear about what is being asked of employees. Instead of trying to manufacture artificial buy-in, leaders can be direct about why it's a condition of employment by having a conversation that inspires self-reflection. Ask: "On a scale of 1 to 10, what is your level of buy-in to this new strategy/change?"

If the employee mentions reservations, expresses resistance, or indicates a low level of buy-in, follow up with questions like "What is your plan to get bought in?" or "How could you use your expertise to mitigate the concerns you have to ensure buy-in and deliver results?"

If buy-in seems out of reach or too daunting for the employee, turn the questions for self-reflection in a different direction: "It sounds like buy-in isn't something you're willing to offer right now. What plans do you have to transition off this assignment or team?"

That question probably will shock an employee who, in all likelihood, wasn't planning on going anywhere. But if you're going to get great results, there can't be an option that allows people to stay and sabotage or to stay and hate. Why would any organization tolerate an option that allows people to generate endless emotional waste? If an employee intends to stick around, the question goes back to "Then what is your plan for buy-in?"

No third option.

Free Up Space for the Willing

Employees who work with great mental processes add value and rarely generate emotional waste. They find a way to move forward quickly and help figure out the "how" after a decision has been made. Otherwise, the option is to step away and free up a space for someone who will.

But don't expect the ego to bow down to this notion. When people are forced to face the fact that buy-in is not negotiable, their next play is going to be an argument: "So my opinion doesn't count?" or "So you want me to be a yes person who goes along with ideas even if I know they won't work?" The ego is expert at emotional blackmail.

When it doesn't feel consulted, the ego has huge tantrums. Why? Because it is a brightly lit sign that the ego isn't in charge and more data that the ego's view of the world is inaccurate. The skills that signal maturity—acceptance, adaptation, evolution—are threatening to the juvenile world of the ego.

Great leaders know, and can make it clear, that they desire the input of employees who are using their thinking, energy, and expertise to move the work forward. Opinions aren't valuable. Action is. Opinions are usually an attempt to stop the action; expertise is used to keep it going. Opinions focus on why we can't. Expertise is at play when employees toward how we can.

In my experience, people with many opinions are often the ones who are light on expertise. Offering opinions is usually a subtle form of resisting change. These people see resistance as the only option that doesn't expose their unreadiness. Leaders who allow that resistance coddle the people who are unwilling to meet and greet reality. Such people haven't yet developed the skills for overcoming barriers.

High-value employees understand the obligation and value of full buy-in even when they haven't been consulted on the decision. In today's world, most decisions are made without consulting everyone who will be affected. They can't be. Consulting everyone is an unrealistic expectation, and it is a bad business practice. To get great at buy-in, people need to get super comfortable with the role of being informed, not consulted. An important Reality-Based Leadership mantra that bypasses ego is "Stay in joy or go in peace."

Preference, Potential, and Personality

Many people don't understand the role of decision making in an organization. We don't work in democracies. The key decision makers are customers, the marketplace, the competition, the regulators, the evidence, best practices, innovation, and breakthroughs. The personal preferences of those working for a company have little to do with what creates competitive advantage outside of the company.

When change is required, people who weren't involved in making a decision often want to assert decision-making authority to not act on it. It's as if they think they have veto power. Change typically is based on opportunity or potential. One of the ways people try to use veto power is by favoring their preferences over the business's potential. The business case is built on a change designed to make something better, to improve processes, relationships with customers, and profits. To threaten a veto because "I don't like it" or "I prefer doing things the old way" is ego. It chooses preference over potential.

NO EGO CORE BELIEF
Personal preference can't trump business potential.

At times, I have asked particularly resistant people why they're resisting. If it's relevant, I ask them, with all the love in my heart, what their signing authority is. And the answer might be "I could spend $1,000 without having to get approval."

But wait a minute, I tell them. "Your preference could cost the organization millions. That is way beyond your signature authority." Personal preference does not trump potential.

I heard a story from a former employee about her former employer. The cafeteria leaders, looking for ways to cut costs and stay in business, decided they didn't have the resources to toast people's bread. They announced that the bread and toasters would be put out so people could toast their own bread. The potential was a big labor cost savings for the cafeteria.

How great is that? People could have fresh, warm toast whenever they wanted, cooked to perfection. The reaction? Mutiny.

The preference was for cafeteria workers to make toast. But everyone had toast-making skills, so the potential savings far outweighed preference.

The ego hates disruption. It loves being conditional and keeping all options open, which lets it off the hook if things get tough. The "conditions" for buy-in give the ego a back-pocket list of reasons, stories, and excuses for why something didn't work out. Conditions justify lack of accountability in case circumstances aren't perfect. In case reality is just too, well, real.

And what has favoring preference really gained anyone? Doing so strokes the ego, provides a temporary feel-good, and gives people the unwarranted luxury of delaying the game. They can procrastinate being ready for what is next.

If leaders allow people to favor preference over potential long enough or often enough, they're in real danger of contributing to the death of competitive advantage. If the business is less competitive, jobs are less secure. And how good will it feel to say "I don't have a job, but, hey, at least I didn't have to change"?

Can't Buy Me Love

As my sons were growing up, I would pick a time to teach them to play poker. I love poker, and I need poker partners for mandatory family fun nights. One of my sons had a harder time catching on than the others. We went over the rules. Then we went over them again. We played practice hand after practice hand. Finally, he had it down. He was ready. I dealt a for-real hand and told everyone to place their bets.

My poker-rookie son hesitated, holding up the game, so I

reminded him that this was the time to place his bet. He refused. "I'm not going to place my bet until I see your cards first," he said.

I laughed. He was like so many people I know, wanting to know the outcome before they would buy in to the game. He wanted to find a way to bend the rules, to up his ante on being able to win. But that's not how poker works, and it's not how life works either. You take the cards you're dealt, and you place the bet based on your skills even though you know you're dealing with the Big Unknown of other people's cards and skills. If you lose a hand or two, you work harder to develop the skills you need to get better. You get coaching and acquire resilience and do what's necessary to build up your emotional bank account. You also can quit playing, but you don't get to stay in the game and demand different rules. The choice for buy-in, especially in the face of past disappointments, signals the skill of resilience. And resilience is a major factor in accountability.

I once worked with a company that had made a decision to use a software sales tool called Salesforce. The business case for using the software was strong. It enables strategic account planning and improved inventory management. It was transparent, so everyone could see all activity on all the accounts. A sale was tracked from opportunity to close, and everyone could see what efforts were driving successful conversions from a lead to a closed deal. Most important, if any given sales rep left, the team would have an understanding of what approaches were working for his or her client and could follow up on anything left in the pipeline.

The software was designed to increase sales, manage

sales accounts nationally and more strategically, cut costs, orchestrate inventory, improve customer experience, and reduce the risk inherent in a top sales rep leaving. Wow. Amazing potential for the business.

Those who'd been keeping up with technology quickly understood the emphasis on strategic account management. It could put an end to the old-school ways of selling that didn't really serve the business—for example, hoarding client contacts and relationships.

In order to capitalize on the great promise of the business case for purchasing the software, everyone needed to quickly become fluent in the new way of working. Don't slow down to be comfortable; speed up to be successful. Full steam ahead, right?

Except for Ed. (Not his real name.)

Ed was dismayed. He wanted an exemption from using the new software. He argued that his 10-year record of successful sales spoke for itself. He preferred to keep his contacts and sales pipeline in an Excel spreadsheet, hidden deep in his hard drive where no one else had access. It worked for him. And if he didn't exactly keep it up to date, it didn't really matter. He kept it all in his head.

The leader, worried about Ed's threats to leave and take customers with him, caved. Ed's blackmail was successful in the sense that he protected his personal preference, but at what cost to the company? The rest of the team was ready to adapt. Why should Ed's comfort level be more important than the vast potential the new software would provide the whole system? It was bad math—forgoing huge potential to the company to accommodate Ed's personal preference. The company suffered just to buy the love of one sales guy.

Here is another way of looking at it. What if your doctor kept prescribing the same blood pressure medicine you'd been taking for 20 years even though new, far more effective drugs were available? Prescribing new drugs would require that the doctor get more educated, read more drug literature, maybe learn new software or a different way to interpret blood tests. With the old drug, no change is required. Sure, your health, quality of life, and longevity potential would get a big boost with the new drugs, but, hey, the doctor has decided preference overrules your potential. If that happened, you'd be furious. Some might even argue malpractice, but no matter what, you'd be shopping for a new doctor.

Strong business cases get whittled away when leaders allow preference to overrule potential. Attempts to create more palatable circumstances stunt people's growth, keep them from stepping up into greatness, and ensure they are even less ready for what's next. Caving in to preference is to wade into an ego-feeding, emotionally wasteful swamp. It's an expensive and unsustainable business practice. Leaders must stop negotiating the nonnegotiables.

The Value of Yes

Most people struggle with saying yes to buy-in because of limited thinking. When we go to say yes, we assume we will have to do all the work. We project that we'll be signing up for an increased workload or a drastic change or some imagined, unwanted impact. Maybe we haven't built up relationships and positive networks, so we believe we will have to do the work single-handedly. No becomes the default that stops us from playing with ideas that lead to innovation and break-through. We focus on why we can't rather than enlisting others and figuring out how we can. We actually need to make saying yes our default whenever possible—at least when it comes to supporting an idea and exploration about how it could become a reality.

Here's a story that illustrates what I mean. When one of my sons was injured during football season, he used his finest ad-olescent logic to conclude that his life was completely over. So I delivered an inspirational parental pep talk on the value of di-versification. He was being presented an opportunity to get fluent in many things so that his source of joy wasn't dependent on one thing. "Discover the theater, music, science fairs, new games . . . anything!" I said. He listened, but I wasn't sure he got the message. Then one Friday night, in the face of extreme boredom, he reminded me of my great diversification discourse and asked if he could attend a theater production that one of his friends was starring in.

I supported my son's willingness to try something new. In fact, I was delighted he was heeding my advice. Even so, the word "no" lingered on the tip of my tongue. I immediately be-gan to project how much work that would mean for me. I have eight sons and have a policy of limiting my chauffeuring trips into town. I had already been twice. I was wearing my comfy lounging clothes, and I was looking forward to a glass of wine and time with my husband, whom I hadn't seen all week.

But then I realized saying no wouldn't serve either of us. My son wouldn't be able to take advantage of the great development advice I'd given, and I would be home with a disappointed teenager. With eight sons, I don't get many nights to myself. And this boy was the only thing between me and a romantic night at home alone with my husband. I said yes instead—but only to his goal of going out.

"I think you should definitely go see this play," I said. "Now let's talk about how you could get there." It was the "yes, *and*" response that demonstrates buy-in. I supported his plan, but I wasn't signing on to heroic efforts to pull it off.

His first suggestion, of course, was that I should drive him. I declined, pointing out I already had made two trips into town, I was in my pajamas, and I had a glass of wine in hand. Then he suggested I pay for Uber. Unfortunately, I told him, because I had a full-time job and own my own car for getting around, I didn't have Uber in my budget.

He rebutted my reasoning, saying his friend's mom was willing to run kids into town any time (an obvious ploy to make me feel guilty about my inferior mothering skills). The guilt play almost worked, but I stayed neutral. "You're right. She does seem willing to help," I said. "Why don't you give her a call?" And he did! She said she'd be happy to pick him up and bring him home.

Saying yes got us both what we wanted. He had his night out at the theater with friends, and I luxuriated in Friday night home alone with my husband.

Those with expertise, business readiness, and a positive network for crowdsourcing are valuable employees because they can say yes to almost anything. They can say yes to driving the goal and then use their resources to figure "the how" that breeds creativity. It's a great practice and a great tool. Saying yes quickly is what gives birth to innovation.

Conclusion

MAKING THE CALL

Some of you may see this leadership approach as tough love. I like to express it a different way: Reality is rough. Leadership is love. As leaders assume their bold new role, one that moves people beyond ego and into endless possibility, let me add a few gentle cautions.

- Check your own ego before you attempt to engage another's.
- Be gentle. You want to wake people up, but not by violently shaking them up.
- Go slowly. Take great care as you disrupt thinking, spur self-reflection, and help people develop the capacity to move more skillfully into reality.
- Make the call to greatness. Work with those willing to answer that call.
- Don't forget: Human potential is limitless. A workplace characterized by consistent creativity, endless innovation, and readiness for what's next is possible. Peace and

happiness in the workplace are achievable. As emotional waste is eliminated, work becomes less effortful and more joyful. Use some of that recaptured energy to celebrate accomplishment and great results.

- Summon up all the compassion you can. We are human. Any of us, at any time, has the ability to move into ego. You will screw this up, but only every day. Forgive yourself. It's a practice. Try again.

- Forgive others early and often. Don't be afraid of the do-over. When you notice the times you could have been better, be transparent: "I reflected on our conversation yesterday and realized that I let you down as a leader. I colluded with you instead of helping you get to a No Ego Moment. I'm sorry. What I wish I had done is this. . . . Can we try again?"

My dream is that one day we'll have signs in our workplaces that say: WARNING. YOUR EGO IS NOT SAFE HERE.

Appendix

REALITY-BASED LEADERSHIP
EGO BYPASS TOOLKIT

Contents

To make it easy for leaders, this appendix is designed to have all the Reality-Based Leadership tools discussed in previous chapters in one easy-to-find place. Here are your tools to break projection, bypass the ego and facilitate great results:

These tools have been used to great effect by thousands of leaders. As discussed in previous chapters, questions are key to effective leadership. Good questions lead to great thinking through self-reflection, which leads to higher consciousness and better mental processes. This process of questions and self-reflection helps shut down the nonproductive and dangerous stories the ego invents. Bypassing ego leads to less emotional waste and better business results.

- What did you do to help?
- What do you know for sure?
- What could you do next to add value?
- What would great look like?
- Are you using your opinion to move the idea forward or to stop the action?
- What would add more value right now, your opinion or your action?
- Would you rather be right or be happy?

Additional Reality-Based Leadership Questions/Phrases

- What should we be doing to help?
- How committed are you?
- Then what did you try?
- What story are you telling yourself right now?
- How do you act when you believe that story?
- What are the facts?
- What would you be doing to help if you didn't have your story?
- What is your goal?
- What has your approach been?
- How is that working for you?
- What would you like to change in your approach?
- What are you committing to?

EDITING YOUR STORY

Writing things down can help you tune in to your thoughts. Writing is especially useful when you are just beginning to use Reality-Based tools and methods and listening to your thoughts is not yet instinctive. Later on, continue to use writing when you've become so enmeshed in a situation that it's hard to stop the automatic, ego-based story loop in your mind. Whenever you are that stressed, it's time to take a break and do this exercise:

1. **Sit down and write what is happening.**

   This is not to share—it's just for you. Don't worry about complete sentences or paragraph structure, grammar, or presentation. Just spew forth and write down exactly what you are thinking.

   Don't edit yourself or judge what you're writing. You could write a paragraph or 10 pages—whatever you need to write; whatever you feel like getting out of your head and onto the page.

2. **Get a highlighter, or just go through and underline every line that you stated as a fact.**

3. Go through each of those "facts" and ask yourself: Do I know that for sure? (Is this really a fact, or is it just part of the story I'm telling myself?)

   Separate the facts from your story as rigorously as you would if you were the editor of a newspaper. Edit out judgment and assumptions, anything you can't absolutely know to be true, anything that you couldn't prove with a source, any assignment of motive, and any premature conclusions.

4. On a separate page, write down the facts that have survived your rigorous questioning.

   You will be left with the things you absolutely know to be true. This is reality. Everything else is your story. Discard, shred, burn, or otherwise drop your story. Focus on the facts—your reality. Ask yourself: What is the very next thing I could do to add value? Take that answer as your simple instructions. Follow through with action.

HELPING OTHERS EDIT THEIR STORIES

You can use this exercise on the fly, with BMW drive-bys, and in one-on-one coaching sessions. Keep white paper and markers handy for this. If you find yourself in a BMW drive-by situation, listen to the upsetting situation people are laying out to you and focus intently on the facts. As you hear one, write it down. At the conclusion of the "story" you have just heard, invite the person to take a look at the paper and read through just the facts. Then ask: "Is this the summary of what we know for sure?" This technique, when conducted with empathy, can take the charge out of a challenging situation, get the person being coached back to neutral, and help him or her to identify what he or she could do next to add value.

WHO NEEDS TO USE THE SBAR?

The SBAR (see worksheet example on page 176) can be used in a variety of situations to structure interactions. It is useful for:

- Anyone who needs to process the story quickly and get to the core of the issue.
- Any leader who wants to make good use of the infamous "You got a minute?"
- Any leader who wants to make sure that an employee has already processed through the story. It can be used as a guide for the employee's thought processes and to bring you up to speed and solicit your help, decisions, and approval in an efficient way.

WHAT IS THE SBAR?

The Situation-Background-Assessment-Recommendations is a mental process model that . . .

- Helps to guide an employee's thinking by eliminating emotional waste in the system.
- Standardizes the thinking process.
- Makes the situation concrete and developmental needs obvious.
- Applies to real-world situations in the moment.
- Provides unique insight into others' thinking.
- Most important, makes the best use of the leader's time and ensures that the work is being done at the appropriate level—it gets you back to leading instead of overmanaging.

WHY USE THE SBAR WITH YOUR TEAM?

When employees bring their SBAR worksheets to you, they will have processed their story—moved out of the drama and really edited down to the facts—using critical thinking to present the situation from a neutral place.

The model provides insight for the leader and opens a window into how employees think, where they need development, and how fluent they are in reality-based thinking. The SBAR keeps employees fact-based and shows them where they need further information from their leader.

Employees and leaders can review multiple SBAR worksheets in a short time frame. Through the leader's review of the SBAR and coaching on each item, employees develop the ability to think in ways that are more aligned with the leader and in ways proven to create great business results.

Over time, employees can collect a series of SBAR worksheets and extract key themes to live by based on their experience of consistent direction from leadership. These SBAR worksheets create a knowledge base for individual employees as well as great case studies to onboard and develop employees. Ultimately, they will expedite consistent decision making throughout the organization.

Use of the SBAR model will conserve energy and focus attention toward solving issues and away from living in the drama. The tool is the key technique in diffusing drama and driving results. It depersonalizes issues and moves people into a professional space where the best ideas can be offered. Eventually, this way of processing information and presenting it efficiently will become intuitive for everyone on the team.

IN-DEPTH SBAR FOR THE LEADER

The SBAR is broken down into four succinct parts and should fit on a single slide or sheet of paper. Each section should be a few sentences at maximum.

SITUATION

The Situation section includes a concise statement of the current situation—the facts, no drama, and minus the symptoms—as brief as a single sentence. It is a straightforward statement that captures what we know for sure about the current state of affairs.

As a leader, when you are looking over this section, ask yourself:

- Is this representation of the situation fact-based? Neutral? Accountable? Straightforward?
- Is this representation accurate? The bottom line? A simple statement of current reality?

BACKGROUND

The Background section includes a concise statement of the relevant background data points that need to be taken into account in deciding how to move forward. When looking over this section, the leader should ask:

- Are any vital pieces of information and history left out?
- Is unnecessary history included that distracts from the facts?
- Are there items that the employee may not be aware of or may be minimizing?

Take the opportunity to enhance the employee's understanding about the many factors influencing the situation.

ASSESSMENT

The Assessment section outlines the author's analysis of the current situation. If the "S" in SBAR is the "WHAT," then the "A" is the "SO WHAT." What difference does it make? Why should people be concerned? What is the root cause? What aren't employees or leaders tending to? What are the main concerns and major risks? What sense should be made of this? This section is about good diagnostics and good interpretation of the situation.

When reviewing this section, leaders have a great opportunity to see an employee's current level of critical thinking skills and to gain insight into his or her problem-solving strengths and weaknesses. Use questions to drive critical thinking. Also, be aware of the tone of the analysis. Ask yourself:

- Is it based on accountability, or is it coming from a place of "victim" thinking or learned helplessness?
- Does it get at the root cause?
- Does the assessment incorporate business insight based on data rather than anecdotes?

If you see development needs here, coach the employee by thinking out loud, asking great questions, and teaching problem-solving techniques.

RECOMMENDATIONS

The Recommendations section contains the action and next steps suggested by the person filling out the SBAR worksheet.

The idea is for the employee to have multiple recommendations. If an employee offers just one recommendation, they are likely to get stuck in "right or wrong" thinking. The recommendations section drives mental flexibility by requiring the employee to offer multiple ways of addressing the issue, each with varying benefits, costs, and risks. Getting in the habit of offering multiple solutions helps people be less judgmental because they realize an issue can be addressed in many ways, and each recommendation has a set of downsides.

These recommendations should be focused on improving or solving the situation with attention to the unique background circumstances. They should be driven by the assessment. When you are looking over this section, leaders should look for the merit of the recommendations. Ask:

- Do the recommendations address the situation?
- Are they feasible?
- Do they match company philosophy and policy?
- Do they balance organizational and customer needs?
- Are they sustainable?
- Are they creative?
- Do they initiate a transactional effort, or could they be transformational?
- What might they jump-start on a process improvement?

Help the employee see creative and multiple options.

NAME:_____

DATE: _____

PROPOSED PROJECT TITLE / ISSUE TITLE:

_____

Note: When making a recommendation, close the loop and make sure both parties agree on the next steps.

SITUATION

What is happening now?

Briefly describe the current situation. Give a clear, succinct overview of the main problem.

_____

_____

_____

_____

BACKGROUND

What relevant factors led up to this event?

Briefly state the pertinent history. What got us to this point? Is this an issue that happens frequently?

_____

_____

_____

_____

_____

THE SBAR MODEL WORKSHEET

ASSESSMENT

What do you think is going on?
What does the data suggest?
What improvements would we see if we made a change?
(Examples: improved efficiency, improved employee morale,
increased customer/client satisfaction, better communication
among staff)

_____

_____

_____

_____

_____

RECOMMENDATIONS

What possible courses of action do you propose?
What actions are you asking for? How can you help make this
change a reality? What is the simplest, fastest, yet most thor-
ough way to make this happen?

_____

_____

_____

_____

_____

FOUR FACTORS OF PERSONAL ACCOUNTABILITY

COMMITMENT

The willingness to do whatever it takes to get the results you desire.

When you are committed, you readily buy in to what is asked of you. What you say and do reflects your true feelings. You have integrity and you are authentic in your interactions with others. No sarcastic or resentful inner voice keeps up a running monologue in your head.

RESILIENCE

The ability to stay the course in the face of obstacles and setbacks.

When you are resilient, you feel calm, purposeful, and confident in your ability to produce results regardless of your circumstances. You do not seriously consider throwing up your hands and quitting or resorting to excuses. If you say you have "tried" to do something, you did not try only one thing. You tried a dozen or more; you persisted, employed problem-solving, and asked for help.

OWNERSHIP

Unwavering acceptance of the consequences of your actions (whether individual or collective), with zero blame or argument.

When you are feeling true ownership, you are able to give the gift of your work unconditionally. You don't look to others to validate your efforts or to absolve you when things go wrong. Your results—good or bad—come because of you, not in spite of you.

CONTINUOUS LEARNING

Seeing both success and failure as fuel for future success.

Developing the ability to learn continuously takes perspective and maturity, and it is its own reward. When you learn from your successes *and* your failures, you are able to let go of seeing as something you are afraid of, something to avoid. You own and use it to get better results in the future. No one ever has succeeded without failures along the way. Holding back your effort out of fear of failure guarantees a lifetime of undue caution and restraint.

DEVELOPING ACCOUNTABILITY THROUGH COACHING

Personal accountability is something everyone has to work on all the time. Building a culture of accountability within your organization is a key element to organizational success. Each individual plays a vital role in a company's success. High-performing organizations are moving toward more empowerment, enlightenment, and organizational accountability, one person at a time.

When faced with conflict, many employees ask questions that can waste resources and lead teams into further dissension. With a single question, one employee can cost the company thousands of dollars, even in cases where the employee has no signature authority to spend money on the company's behalf. A single resistance-based question can tie up resources in the form of meetings, research, analysis, and discussions that waste time, talent, and focus. Key resources are wasted seeking an answer that doesn't exist, doesn't matter, or reinforces the erroneous belief that others are the source of problems.

THE ACCOUNTING-FOR EXERCISE

To promote continuous learning, it is important to make a practice of highlighting day-to-day results produced by the team. If the team had great results, ask each employee to account for the decisions, choices, approaches, and behaviors that led to success so that each person can intentionally duplicate them. If the team's results were lackluster, ask each employee to identify ways in which he or she personally contributed. Responses must begin with strong "I" statements that reflect accountability, such as "I chose," "I denied," "I assumed," "I did," "I didn't," and "I acted." (See the series of questions in the following list.) Once each person identifies his or her specific contributions, positive and negative, the individual can commit to what he or she will do differently next time. This facilitates individual development and better future results.

Questions to ask when accounting for results:

- What were your results?
- Did you succeed or not? (Watch for the individual or team that lowers the standard, wanting to believe that they "did pretty well considering the circumstances," as if they should get extra points for challenges.)
- What happened? (Listen for employee stories; are individuals accounting for the facts and their behaviors?)
- How do you account for your results? (Listen for "I," not "we," "they," or "you.")

- What did you believe?
- How did that belief affect your behavior, attitude, creativity, and choices?
- What were the facts? What did you know or what do we know for sure?
- How committed were you? How bought in were you?
- What could you change to ensure your success in the future? (Make sure changes are stated in the first person and don't hinge on having more resources, changing others, or changing reality and circumstances.)
- What are you committing to in the future? (Have the employee write it down. This is his or her new development plan. And then hold him or her to it.)

BRINGING ACCOUNTABILITY INTO THE PROCESS

Employee engagement action planning with your team is an excellent opportunity to introduce greater accountability and foster engagement and great results. Here's how:

1. Share the results of the engagement survey with your team.

2. Hang three large flip chart pages in front of the group.

3. Ask team members to specifically name the ways they would like to improve the work environment. Write the ideas down on the first sheet of paper.

4. Once the list is complete, ask team members what they are willing to do to improve the workplace in these areas. Record their comments on the second sheet of paper. The list should be specific and focused on what employees or teams can do to impact their own circumstances. This is where accountability is cultivated and employees begin to take responsibility for their own engagement.

5. Last, ask group members what support they need from you, as their manager, or from the organization. List these things on the third sheet.

Check to see if the tasks and ideas listed on the second and third sheets are robust enough to create the type of workplace outlined on the first sheet. If not, spend more time working on those lists, particularly the second one focused on how employees can affect their own circumstances.

1. Create action plans for the ideas employees are willing to invest in to affect their own circumstances. Add in timelines and responsibilities, and communicate back to the group both the initial work and the progress made.

2. Host regular check-in meetings.

HIRING FOR ACCOUNTABILITY

Organizations can avoid a drama epidemic and emotional waste by developing better hiring practices. Companies can improve efficiency, unleash human potential, and turn excuses into results by incorporating personal accountability into the typical behavioral interviewing process.

KEY POINTS

Candidates who have high personal accountability . . .

- Believe that results happen because of their actions, not in spite of them; that they choose their own destiny.
- Are committed to doing whatever it takes.
- Demonstrate perseverance in the face of obstacles.
- Are great problem-solvers.
- Have the ability to stay the course in the face of setbacks.
- Exhibit ownership of their results.
- Show unwavering acceptance of the consequences of their actions.
- Do not blame others.
- Learn from their results.
- Are able to identify and account for their part in outcomes and to turn learning into development plans, new competencies, and future results.

Ask the following types of questions to find out a candidate's fluency in each of the four factors of accountability:

Willingness/Commitment. Ask people to tell you about a time when they were asked to do something outside of their job description. Let them tell the story, and then ask how they responded or how they made sense of the request. The best answers sound like "I get asked to do things outside my job description all the time. I am here to do what is needed in the moment."

Resilience. Ask candidates about a time when they were given a task that seemed impossible. Listen for how they approached the barriers. A follow-up question may be "In hindsight, do you think you could have done anything differently?"

Ownership. Ask them about a failure at work and about their part in it. Listen for the use of "I." And listen to see if they learned to adjust their behaviors based on what they learned.

Continuous Learning. Use these questions to determine whether a candidate is focused on learning—especially in the case of failure.

- What did you learn?
- Have you applied your learnings in different situations since then? If so, how?

Decline candidates demonstrating these tendencies:

- Attempting one approach and then quitting.
- Expecting others to make situations easier.
- Resenting circumstances or other people.
- Needing validation from others to do their best.

A Conversational Guide to Assess Personal Accountability

- Describe a time when you worked with a boss who didn't support you.
- Tell me about a time when you were coached on subpar performance.
- Tell me about a time when a peer or a direct report did not pull his/her weight on your team.
- Describe a time when you presented two different opinions of one situation because of the audience.
- Describe a time when you accepted blame for a failure.

NEGATIVE BRAINSTORMING EXERCISE

One of the most useful tools for transitioning a team from resistance to success, regardless of circumstances, is called "negative brainstorming." You'll need a whiteboard or a large flip chart to get started. Here's how it works:

1. Introduce the exercise and explain the rules: Each individual can introduce his or her concerns, one at a time, in front of the group, while you write them down. (Leave ample space beside each concern for the next step in the exercise.) Other group members must refrain from discussion, critique, or disagreement and wait their turns. Continue until all of the group's concerns have been documented.

2. Title the list of concerns "Risks." Point out that concerns are simply risks. The true power of the team lies in its ability to mitigate risks. This idea is at the heart of the exercise, and it's the reason it works.

3. Taking it risk by risk, ask the team to honestly evaluate the probability of each risk manifesting. Assign each risk a probability of high, medium, or low and label it. Next, evaluate the potential impact of each risk and again label it high, medium, or low.

4. Now comes the negative brainstorming. Redirect the energy the team was putting into resistance or dissent into creating strategies to mitigate each risk labeled

"high" or "medium" in probability or impact. Write down the strategies for mitigation.

This exercise helps teams use their expertise to make things work as opposed to editorializing and resisting. This will position them as valuable assets and credible witnesses. That's why getting negative with your team can be positive—but only in the service of moving things forward, creating great results, and succeeding in spite of challenging circumstances.

ISSUES ---> RISKS	PROBABILITY			IMPACT		
1. Example: We don't have enough resources to manage this.	H	M	~~L~~	H	M	~~L~~
2.	H	M	L	H	M	L
3.	H	M	L	H	M	L
4.	H	M	L	H	M	L
5.	H	M	L	H	M	L
6.	H	M	L	H	M	L

This exercise shows your faith not only in the team members' talents but also in their good intentions. Negative brainstorming provides Reality-Based leaders a constructive way to air concerns and gives dissent a place within a healthy team dynamic. It's an especially great tool to keep leading constructively even when your company has done something you, the leader, don't like or disagree with. It can be tempting to stop leading under those circumstances, but your responsibility is to redirect focus. (You go first!) In the end, it's about the overarching vision of what you have joined together to create, because risks are here to stay. Your perspective is what matters.

After having been encouraged to think outside the box for many years, you may have come to overuse this competency or use it at inappropriate times. The time for thinking outside the box is during strategic planning efforts or business process reengineering efforts.

Consistently ignoring your organization's constraints and offering out-of-the-box thinking to problem-solving efforts is a mistake. You will come to be seen as a dreamer or someone out of touch with reality.

Instead of thinking about what shouldn't be happening or the ideal situation, recognize and accept your company's goals and constraints (such as a hiring freeze or limited funding) and think *inside that box*. The constraints are real—wishing them away won't help—but you can propose solutions that address them while also serving your goals. Again, think in terms of "and," not "or." By doing this, you will be offering real solutions that respect the very real constraints you currently face.

GOAL

CONSTRAINT 1

SOLUTIONS
"How I / We Can . . ."

CONSTRAINT 2

Power of "And" Exercise

When you see that employees are wishing away their current reality and need to instead imagine ways in which they could achieve goals within the given constraints, try this step-by-step exercise, moving employees away from a sense of lack and impossibility, and toward a focus on solutions.

1. Identify the goal or goals.
2. Identify the constraints or competing needs.
3. Box it out.
4. Replace "or" with "and."
5. Problem solve.

Think of decisions as investments. You put time and energy into them—and sometimes money too. The more you invest in making a decision, the more likely it is that you will make the best possible decision. But sometimes the distance between the best-possible decision and the worst-possible decision is not great, or the stakes in the decision are not very high. In such a case, you certainly do not want to invest a lot of resources in the decision.

TOOLS FOR THE NEW LEADERSHIP ROLE

How does a leader begin to facilitate introspection and reflection that will help others bypass ego to fertilize growth and development? It's not as complex or difficult as you might think. Have a list of great questions, be ready to use them right after giving feedback, and give employees time to process the question and their stories. Here is a list of recommended questions, followed by more formal assignments for self-reflection:

- What are you trying to create?
- What do you want? What are you willing to do to get that?
- What do you fear that is getting in the way of action? How can you move beyond that fear or concern?
- What are some of the most challenging parts of your role? What do you wish you were more skilled or more fluent in handling?
- What part of our reality are you struggling with?
- What would happen if you just choose to agree and help?
- What would be your part in that outcome?
- What did you do that hindered progress or success? What helped?
- What do you know for sure?
- What could you do to add value?

- If you didn't have the story you're telling yourself right now, who would you be?
- What is your goal?
- How is that working for you?
- What has your current approach been? What would you like to change in that approach?
- How is the feedback I gave you true?
- If we assume the universe is kind, how might this situation be benefiting you or be for your highest good?
- What would make this successful, and what will you do to ensure that?
- If there were other explanations for someone's behavior, what might they be?
- What is missing from this situation? What could you do to add to it?
- What if two things are true? Where is the "and" here?

ASSIGNMENTS FOR SELF-REFLECTION

Here are suggested assignments for self-reflection we've used to great effect in Reality-Based Leadership. These assignments are a way to crowdsource employee feedback and generate input from diverse perspectives. The philosophy behind these assignments is self-study, asking yourself questions about yourself, getting quiet as you think about the answers, finding clarity about what is true and where the ego narrator in your head is leading you astray. Insights bubble up in these conversations. Leaders become the facilitators of the self-learning. Meditation and journaling can be great supports.

Ask or tell employees:

- Whom do you know who is generally successful under these kinds of circumstances? Connect with them, ask for their three best tips on how to be successful, and let's talk about what you learn.
- Get a clearer picture of how others experience you in meetings by using your phone or tablet to record your interactions. Watch the film and identify ways you use your body language, approach or speech to diminish open dialogue.
- In one clear sentence, write down what you hope to accomplish or create in these circumstances. Talk to 20 people and ask them for a next step or their best tip on how to proceed. Work from that list and report back with your experience next week.

- Think about three ways this feedback could be true. Come back and share three examples of how it affected your work.

- Identify three ways that you sabotaged the work efforts. How did your actions serve you?

- What thoughts are you believing? How is that influencing your choices and actions?

- Choose three people who excel in this area and interview them. Report back with what you discover.

- Write down a reality we're currently experiencing or a decision that has just been made. On a sheet of paper, write: "And this means that . . . ," then make a list of what it means. Take a look at your list and ask, "Do you know this to be true? Can you impact this in a positive way? How might you be wrong? How does this kind of thinking keep you stuck?"

- Listen to the ego narrator in your head. Capture a day's worth of thoughts on paper. What do you notice? What themes do you see? Examine thoughts that express certainty about the future or are rooted in the past. When we reconnect, we'll talk about what sense you make of them.

- Read [a book or article] or watch [a video, TED Talk, etc.]. Identify two things that resonate with you. Afterward, let's talk about why you found those things important.

Index

cafeteria management
     example, 152–3
Cappelli, Peter, 23
challenge, 101, 106
change management, 18, 22,
     116–32
  and bold new thinking, 122
  and "change is hard,"
     123–5
  and the ego, 153
  and emotional waste,
     120–1
  and feeling overwhelmed,
     128–9
  and grief, 125–7
  and initiatives, 128–9
  myths of, 123–30
  is outdated, 116–20
  and pace, 129–30
  traditional, 131–2
  See also business
     readiness
choices, 6, 12, 24, 42–4,
     53–4, 62–6, 72,
     83–4, 98, 101, 107–9,
     114, 141, 149, 154,
     181–2, 195
  and accountability, 98
  and buy-in, 149, 154
  and engagement, 62–6
  and greatness, 12
  and locus of control, 83–4

and motivation, 6, 42–4
and paper writing, 72
and results, 24
and self-reflection, 53–4
circumstances, 39, 71–4, 82
  and accountability, 82
  difficult, 71–4
coaching, 3, 6–12, 34, 44, 86,
     90–6, 114, 129, 136–8,
     149, 154, 165, 168, 171,
     174, 180, 187
  and accountability, 180
  and buy-in, 149
  conversations, 136–7
  and feedback, 34
  and great coaching
     questions, 165
  and "greatness," 8–12
  and "group coaching," 114
coddling, 20, 32, 92, 120–3,
     128, 148, 151
cognitive therapy, 5
collegial mentoring, 101,
     110–11
commitment, 101–2, 135–7,
     178
comparisons, 25, 35
"compassion fatigue," 37–8
complaining, 15, 25, 35, 41,
     59, 67, 70–4, 87–91,
     122–8, 134, 138, 141
  See also BMW

and the ego, 28–39

and journaling, 108

questions, 38–9, 51–3, 108,
    135, 139–40, 149–50,
    192–4

and timing, 50

and venting, 28

"sense-making mentoring,"
    110–11

silent majority, 137–9,
    143–4

situation (and SBAR model),
    173

skill development, 128,
    153–4

smartphones, 124–5

status quo, 118

"Stay in joy or go in peace,"
    48, 151

"Stop Believing Everything
    You Think," 41, 44–5,
    109

"Stop Guessing and Inquire,"
    49

"Stop Judging, Start
    Helping," 4, 46–7

stories (ego's), 2–5, 16, 21,
    28–31, 34, 44–8, 52,
    56–61, 77–8, 104,
    108–10, 141–2, 152–3,
    166–8

and ambiguity, 56

disrupting, 44–8

editing, 5, 60–1, 141–2

and New Story Exercise,
    166–8

and projecting, 16

and "storks bring babies,"
    77–8

and suffering, 30–1

versus reality, 30, 44

See also projection

"storks bring babies" story,
    77–8

stress, 31, 45, 50–1, 63,
    166

suffering, 23, 26, 30–1,
    35–41, 44, 55, 121–6

and attachment, 121

and the ego, 26

is self-imposed, 23

and stories, 30–1

suspicion, 46–9, 55

sympathy versus empathy,
    36–8, 121–2, 128

"Take Your Own Advice," 49

tattling, 2–4, 25, 99

therapist perspective, 1, 5,
    21–2, 55, 63

thinking inside the box,
    59–60, 190–1